McGraw-Hill Reading
WonderWorks

W9-AVW-847

Mc
Graw
Hill
Education

Bothell, WA • Chicago, IL • Columbus, OH • New York, NY

Cover and Title Page: Nathan Love

mheducation.com/prek-12

Send all inquiries to:
McGraw-Hill Education
Two Penn Plaza
New York, New York 10121

ISBN: 978-0-02-129795-5
MHID: 0-02-129795-9

Printed in the United States of America.

11 QVS 21 20 19 18 17

D

Program Authors

Douglas Fisher

Jan Hasbrouck

Timothy Shanahan

Bothell, WA • Chicago, IL • Columbus, OH • New York, NY

Growing and Learning

The Big Idea

(t to b) John Hovell; Richard Johnson

Go Digital! www.connected.mcgraw-hill.com

Figure It Out

The Big Idea

Go Digital! www.connected.mcgraw-hill.com

(t to b) © Richard Hutchings/Corbis; ©EpicStockMedia/Alamy; Dara Goldman

Unit 3

One of a Kind

The Big Idea

(t to b) Jago Silver; Peter Ferguson

Go Digital! www.connected.mcgraw-hill.com

4

Meet the Challenge

The Big Idea

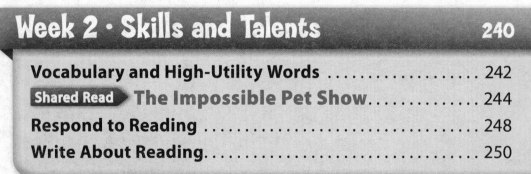

(t to b) B Gerardo Suzan; Marcin Piwowarski

Unit 5

TAKE ACTION

The Big Idea

(t to b) Melissa McGill; Chris Vallo

Go Digital! www.connected.mcgraw-hill.com

(t to b) Frank Leonhardt/dpa picture alliance archive/Alamy Stock Photo; Arthur Schatz/Time & Life Pictures/Getty Images; Holger Burmeister/Alamy

Unit 6

Think It Over

The Big Idea

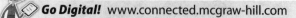 **Go Digital!** www.connected.mcgraw-hill.com

10

A C T
Access Complex Text

Some text can be hard to understand. It can be complex. But you can figure it out! Take notes as you read. Then ask yourself questions.

Vocabulary

☐ Did I look for context clues to help me figure out words I don't know?

☐ Did I use a dictionary to look up words and terms?

Make Connections

☐ Did I connect ideas from one part of the text to another?

Text Features

☐ Are there illustrations or photos that help me understand the text?

☐ Is there a map or a diagram that gives me information?

Text Structure

☐ Did I look at how the text is organized?

☐ What kinds of sentences are in the text and what do they tell me?

Mike Moran

Text Evidence

The details in the text are the clues that will help you answer a question. These clues are called text evidence. Sometimes you will find answers right there in text. Sometimes you need to look in different parts of the text.

It's Stated – Right There!

☐ Can I find the answer in one sentence?

☐ Do I need to look for details in more than one place in the text?

☐ Did I use the text evidence to answer the question?

It's Not Stated – But Here's My Evidence

☐ Did I look for important clues in the text?

☐ Did I use the clues to answer the question?

Talk About It

Talking with your classmates is a great way to share ideas and learn new things. Have a good idea? Share it! Not sure about something? Ask a question!

When I Talk

- ☐ Did I use complete sentences?
- ☐ Did I talk about one topic and describe the key details?
- ☐ Did I speak clearly?

When I Listen

- ☐ Did I listen carefully when others spoke?
- ☐ If I didn't understand something, did I ask a question?
- ☐ Did I ask questions about the topic so I could learn more?

Discussion Rules
- ☑ Be respectful.
- ☑ Speak one at a time.
- ☑ Listen to others with care.

Mike Moran

Write About Reading

A good way to think about what you have read is to write about it. You can write to tell what you think. You can write to share what you learned. Use evidence from the text to support your ideas and opinions.

Getting Ready to Write

☐ Did I look back at my notes about what I read?

☐ Did I find text evidence to support my opinions or ideas?

Writing Opinions

☐ Did I tell my opinion with a topic sentence?

☐ Did I use text evidence to support my opinion?

☐ Did I end with a strong conclusion?

Writing Informative Texts

☐ Did I start with a clear topic sentence?

☐ Did I use facts and definitions from the text to develop my topic?

☐ Did I end with a strong conclusion?

Unit
1

Growing and Learning

The Big Idea

How can learning help us grow?

18

Write words that tell about what you have learned by reading stories.

Stories

Self control

Be yourself

Describe something you learned by reading. Use words from above.

Inti St Clair/Blend Images/Getty Images

Vocabulary

 Work with a partner to complete each activity.

1 improved

List two things that can be *improved* with practice.

_____

2 educated

Tom was *educated* and learned about space at science camp.

Read the sentence above out loud. What words help you understand what *educated* means?

_____

3 effort

Look around the classroom. Write one thing that would take a lot of *effort* to lift.

_____

4 concentrate

Circle two things you need to *concentrate* to do.

read　　play　　study　　sleep

5 ached

Joe's legs *ached* after he ran the race. Write two words that mean almost the same as *ached*.

_____

_____

6 inspired

Aunt May *inspired* Lisa to write a poem. Name one thing you are *inspired* to do.

_____

7 satisfied

These words mean almost the same as *satisfied*. Add another word to the list.
satisfied: thrilled, pleased

_____

8 discovery

Draw a *discovery* you might find on a hike in the woods.

High-Frequency Words

▶ **Read** each word. **Spell** each word. **Write** each word.

and _____

was _____

the _____

place _____

around _____

help _____

Read the story. **Circle** the high-frequency words.

Bill (and) Dad went camping. Their tent was in the best place. Bill and Dad walked around the lake. What a great trip!

My Notes

Read "Bruno's New Home." Use this page to take notes as you read.

_____

_____

_____

_____

_____

_____

_____

_____

_____

_____

_____

BRUNO'S NEW HOME

Essential Question

What can stories teach you?

Read about how one story taught a bear an important lesson.

Bruno shivered. It was almost winter and he was cold. He had to find a warm place to sleep.

Bruno walked around. Finding a new home was hard. No place was right. Then he made a **discovery**.

Text Evidence

1 Comprehension
Character

Reread the first paragraph. **Circle** the name of the main character. What does he need?

a HOMe

Underline the text evidence.

2 Expand Vocabulary

At the beginning of the story, Bruno **shivered**. **Draw a box** around the words that help you understand what *shivered* means.

3 Genre ACT

Look at the illustration on page 22. Name two things that help you know this story is a fantasy.

He has a hat.

23

Text Evidence

8/15/23

1 Expand Vocabulary

An **entrance** is an opening. Why was the *entrance* to the cave too small?

block too

_____

_____

2 Genre A C T

Reread this page. **Draw a box** around one thing that Bruno can do that real bears can't.

3 Comprehension
Character

Reread the last paragraph. Why do Bruno's paws ache and hurt?

He dugg and

_____

dug.

_____

Circle the text evidence.

24

Bruno saw a cave. The **entrance** was too small. It was blocked by dirt and roots.

"I can dig out the dirt and rip out the roots," said Bruno.

Bruno dug and dug. It took a lot of hard work and **effort**. His paws **ached** and hurt. He was tired. Then he heard a loud sound.

Bruno saw a small squirrel eating a nut.

Bruno sighed. "This is **hopeless**. I will never get into my new home."

"I'm Jack, and I can help," said the squirrel.

"But you are too small," said Bruno.

Jack told Bruno to rest. He ran off. A few minutes later, Jack came back.

Text Evidence

1 Expand Vocabulary

If you think something is **hopeless**, you think it cannot be done. Reread the second paragraph.

Draw a box around the sentence that tells why Bruno feels *hopeless*.

2 Comprehension
Character

Reread this page. List two words that describe Jack.

Kind

hopful

Circle the text evidence that supports your answers.

3 Genre A C T

Underline a sentence that shows this story is a fantasy.

Text Evidence

1 Genre ACT

Look at the illustration. **Draw a box** around something that could not happen in real life.

2 Comprehension
Character

Reread the first paragraph. Why does Bruno put on his glasses?

_____

_____

3 Comprehension
Character

Reread the second paragraph. Is Bruno more like the lion or the mouse in the story?

_____

Circle the text evidence.

Jack gave Bruno a book. Bruno put on his glasses. He wanted to **concentrate** on the story.

The story was about a lion and a mouse. The lion gets caught in a net. He doesn't think the mouse can help. But the mouse chews the net and helps the lion.

Bruno was **inspired**. Jack had sharp teeth like the mouse. Jack could help.

Jack and Bruno worked together. Jack chewed the roots. Bruno dug. Finally, Bruno could fit in his new cave.

"Your snug home is **cozy** and warm," said Jack.

"Yes. I am **satisfied** and happy," said Bruno. "I also learned that friends can come in all sizes."

Text Evidence

1 Comprehension
Character

Reread the second paragraph. How does Jack help Bruno get what he needs?

_____

_____

Circle the text evidence.

2 Expand Vocabulary

Underline two words that help you understand what **cozy** means.

3 Genre ACT

Reread the fourth paragraph. What lesson does Bruno learn?

_____

Draw a box around the text evidence.

27

Respond to Reading

Discuss Work with a partner. Use the discussion starters to answer the questions about "Bruno's New Home." Write the page numbers.

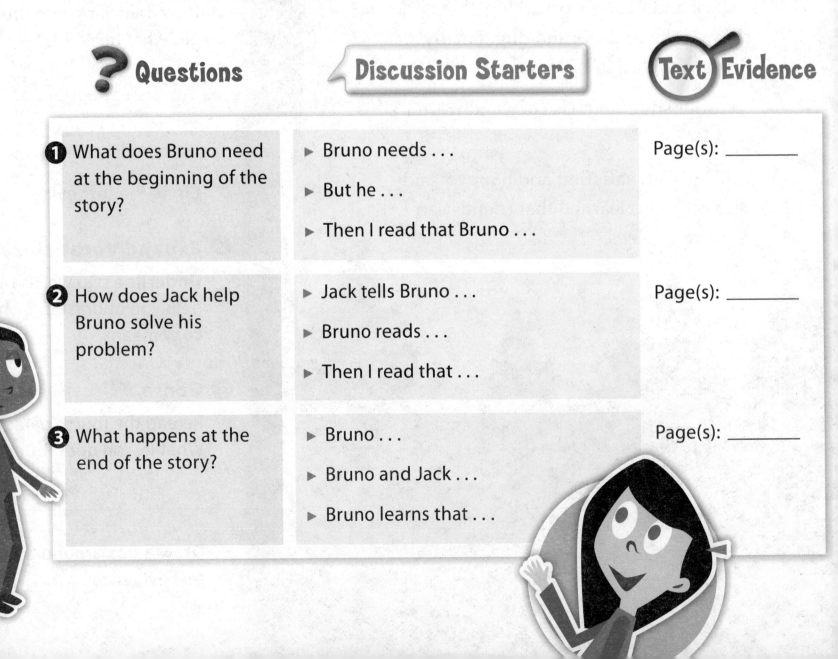

? Questions

Discussion Starters

Text Evidence

1 What does Bruno need at the beginning of the story?

▶ Bruno needs . . .

▶ But he . . .

▶ Then I read that Bruno . . .

Page(s): _____

2 How does Jack help Bruno solve his problem?

▶ Jack tells Bruno . . .

▶ Bruno reads . . .

▶ Then I read that . . .

Page(s): _____

3 What happens at the end of the story?

▶ Bruno . . .

▶ Bruno and Jack . . .

▶ Bruno learns that . . .

Page(s): _____

Write Review your notes. Then use text evidence to answer the question below.

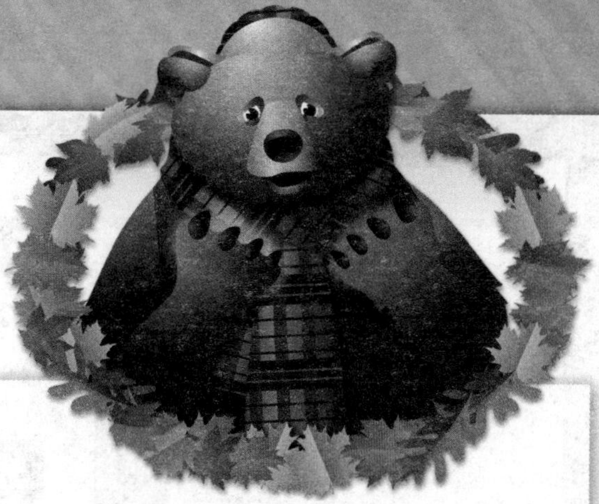

How does a story teach Bruno an important lesson?

In the beginning of the story, Bruno ______________________________

____

____

Then he ______________________________

____

The story helps Bruno ______________________________

____

____

Bruno learns that ______________________________

____

____

John Hovell

Write About Reading

Shared Read

Read an Analysis **Character** Read Eric's paragraph about "Bruno's New Home." He analyzes how the author uses what Bruno does and says to tell the story.

Student Model

Topic Sentence

Circle the topic sentence. What does Eric tell?

Evidence

Draw a box around the text evidence. Is there any other evidence in the story Eric could tell about?

Concluding Statement

Underline the concluding statement. Why is it a good way to end the paragraph?

In "Bruno's New Home," the author does a good job showing how a story helps Bruno learn a lesson. At the beginning of the story, Bruno needs help. Jack gives Bruno a book. The book helps Bruno see that Jack can help. The author uses a story to help Bruno learn that friends can come in all sizes.

Leveled Reader

In _____

I think the author_____

_____

For example, the author uses _____

_____

_____

The author also _____

_____

I think the author _____

_____

_____

Topic Sentence

☐ Include the title of the text you read.

Evidence

☐ Tell how the author uses what the character says and does.

☐ Give examples.

Concluding Statement

☐ Restate how the author uses what the character says and does to teach a lesson.

Talk About It

Essential Question

What can traditions teach you about cultures?

Go Digital!

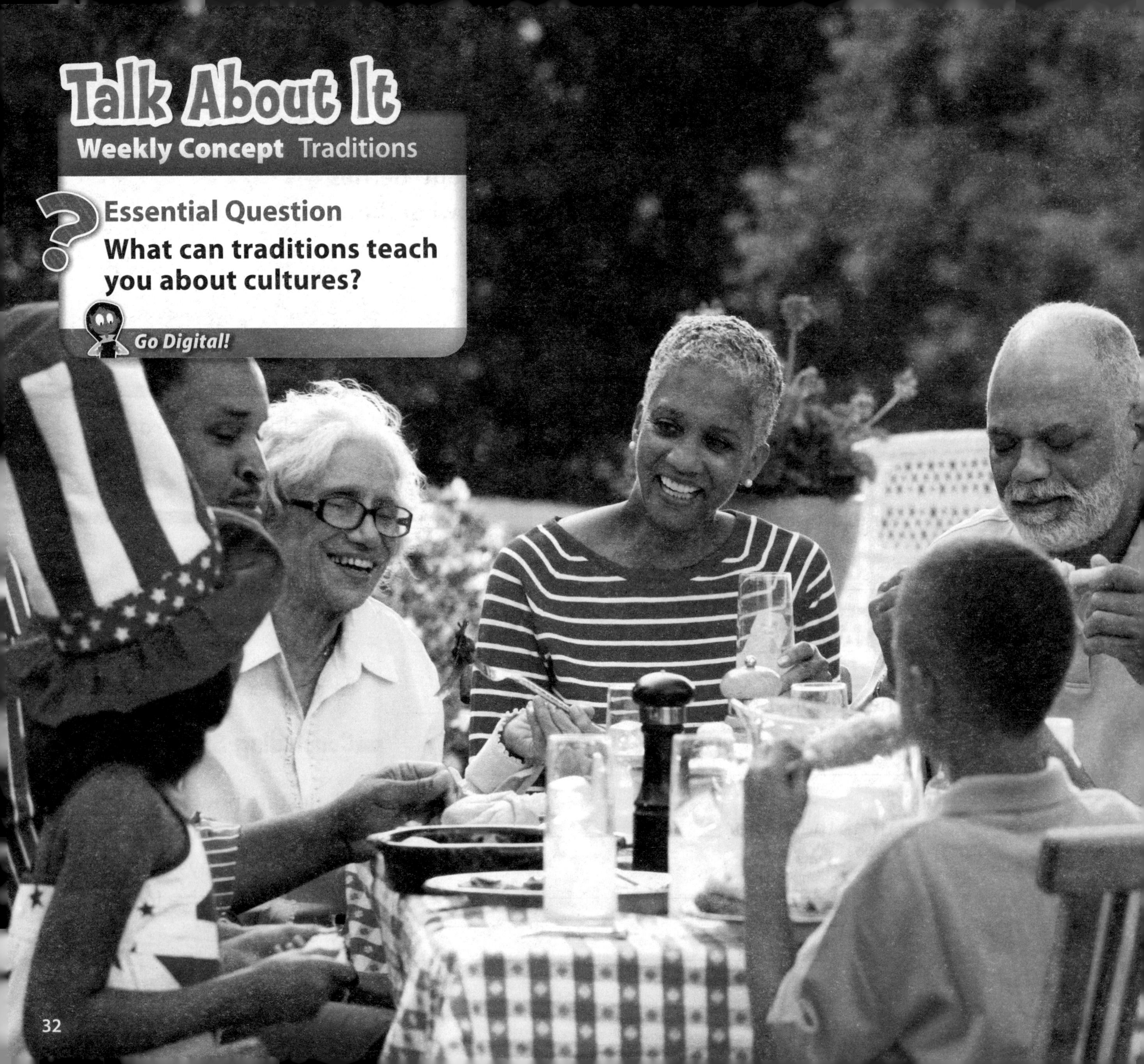

32

Write words that tell about a family tradition.

We go camping in the summer.

We celebrate Christmas together.

Traditions

 Tell about your family tradition. Use words you wrote above.

Vocabulary

❶ tradition

Mark's favorite *tradition* is his family's Fourth of July picnic. What is your favorite *tradition*?

I like going to Christmas Eve service and opening presents.

❷ celebrate

Jen and Dave *celebrate* and cheer when their team wins. What word means almost the same as *celebrate*?

cheer

❸ symbols

The flag and the Statue of Liberty are *symbols* of America. Circle two more *symbols* of our country.

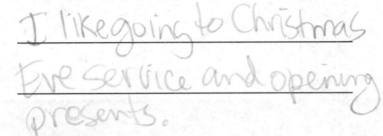

flower   (star)   boat

(eagle)   crayon   cake

❹ courage

It takes *courage* to be a police officer. What is something that you have to do that takes *courage*?

_____

❺ disappointment

Missing your class trip is a big *disappointment*. Show how you might look if you were disappointed.

❻ pride

Ben felt *pride* when he learned to hit a baseball.

Read the sentence above out loud. When do you feel *pride*?

When friends and family visit me.

8/18/23

34

hĕr / hēre

7 **remind**

Name one thing your teacher always has to *remind* you to do.

_____

8 **precious**

Draw something that is *precious* to you.

High-Frequency Words

▶ **Read** each word. **Spell** each word. **Write** each word.

can _can_____

her _her_____

this _this_____

from _from_____

for _for_____

you _you_____

Read the story. **Circle** the high-frequency words.

My grandma (can) cook. (Her) soup is the best. She makes it for me. I want to learn from her. (You) should try it!

Read "The Dream Catcher." Use this page to take notes as you read.

_____

_____

_____

_____

_____

_____

_____

_____

_____

_____

_____

_____

Shared Read > Genre • Realistic Fiction

The Dream Catcher

Essential Question

What can traditions teach you about cultures?

Read how Peter learns about his culture.

Peter walked home from school. Tears ran down his face.

"What's wrong?" said Peter's grandmother. Peter called her Nokomis. It was the Ojibwe name for grandmother.

"I have to give a **presentation**," said Peter. "It is a short talk. I have to tell about a family **tradition**. I know we have lots of customs. I can't think of any. Can you **remind** me?

"Come with me," said Nokomis.

Text Evidence

1 Comprehension

Sequence

How does Peter feel at the beginning of the story?

Sad

Underline the text evidence that supports your answer.

2 Sentence Structure A C T

The author uses dialog to tell the story. What does Nokomis ask Peter when she sees he is upset? **Circle** it.

3 Expand Vocabulary

Reread the third paragraph. What is a **presentation**?

short talk

Draw a box around the text evidence.

Richard Johnson

37

Text Evidence

8/22/23

❶ Comprehension
Sequence

Underline what Peter does after Nokomis gives him the box. What happens next?

_____

_____

❷ Expand Vocabulary

Reread the third paragraph. What word helps you figure out what **woven** means?

tied

❸ Sentence Structure (A)(C)(T)

Read the last sentence. What word tells you how the dream catcher makes Peter feel?

_____

Peter followed Nokomis. She gave him a small box.

"Open it," she said.

Peter opened the box. He saw a wooden hoop. It had string **woven**, or tied, around the circle. It looked like a spider web. There were feathers and beads.

Peter smiled.

Richard Johnson

"This is a dream catcher," said Nokomis. "It is a family tradition and part of our culture. We are strong. The circles are **symbols** of **strength**. We will hang it by your bed. It can catch bad dreams while you sleep. It will give you **courage** and make you feel brave."

"Can I take this one to school?" asked Peter.

"No," said Nokomis.

Text Evidence

1 Expand Vocabulary

Reread the first paragraph. **Draw a box around** the word that means almost the same thing as **strength**.

2 Sentence Structure Ⓐ Ⓒ Ⓣ

What does Nokomis tell Peter they will do with the dream catcher?

_____

_____

3 Comprehension
Sequence

What does Peter want to do with the dream catcher?

_____

_____

Underline the text evidence.

Text Evidence

1 Comprehension
Sequence

Reread the first paragraph. What do Nokomis and Peter do?

_____

Underline the text evidence.

2 Comprehension
Sequence

What happens as Peter falls asleep?

_____

_____

Underline the text evidence.

3 Sentence Structure ⒶⒸⓉ

Reread the second paragraph. **Circle** what Peter wants to do.

Nokomis and Peter made a dream catcher. As Peter fell asleep, he looked at the dream catcher over his bed and made a plan.

"I am going to show my class how to make a dream catcher," said Peter.

Nokomis loved the idea. "Let's **celebrate** after your presentation," she said. "I will bake corn cookies!"

Peter shared his dream catcher. He wasn't **nervous** or scared. He felt brave. He also felt **pride** in himself. He was happy.

Text Evidence

1 Sentence Structure **ACT**

Reread the first paragraph. **Circle** the sentence that shows Nokomis is excited. Then read the sentence aloud.

2 Expand Vocabulary

What word means almost the same as **nervous**?

_____

Draw a box around it.

3 Comprehension
Sequence

How does Peter feel at the end of the story?

_____

Underline the text evidence.

Richard Johnson

41

Respond to Reading

COLLABORATE

Discuss Work with a partner. Use the discussion starters to answer the questions about "The Dream Catcher." Write the page numbers.

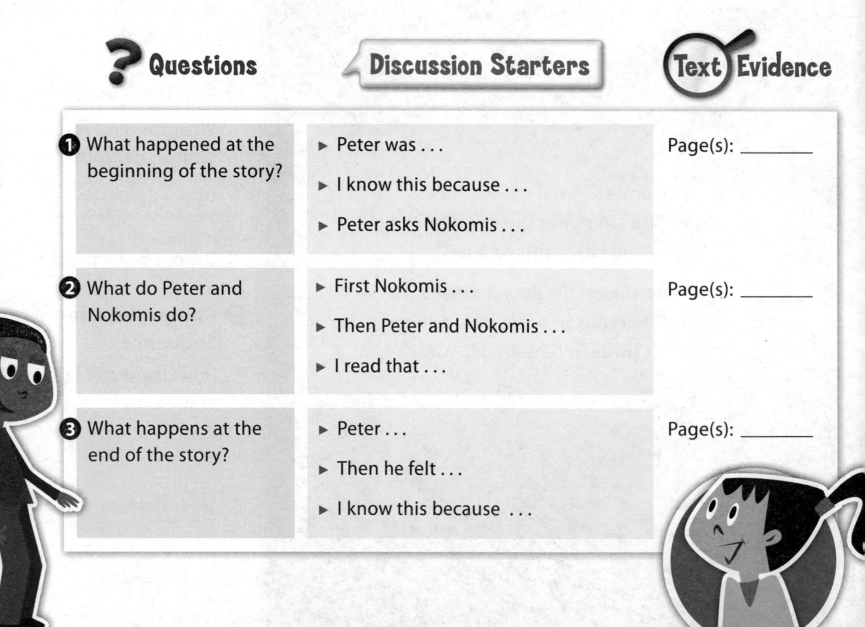

? Questions

Discussion Starters

Text Evidence

1. What happened at the beginning of the story?
   - ▶ Peter was . . .
   - ▶ I know this because . . .
   - ▶ Peter asks Nokomis . . .

   Page(s): _____

2. What do Peter and Nokomis do?
   - ▶ First Nokomis . . .
   - ▶ Then Peter and Nokomis . . .
   - ▶ I read that . . .

   Page(s): _____

3. What happens at the end of the story?
   - ▶ Peter . . .
   - ▶ Then he felt . . .
   - ▶ I know this because . . .

   Page(s): _____

Write Review your notes. Then use text evidence to answer the question below.

What does the dream catcher teach Peter about his culture?

At the beginning of the story, Peter _____

_____

_____

First Nokomis _____

_____

_____

Then she and Peter _____

_____

At the end of the story, Peter _____

_____

_____

Write About Reading

Shared Read

Read an Analysis **Sequence** Read Ashley's paragraph about "The Dream Catcher." She analyzes how the author uses what Peter and Nokomis do and say to tell the events in the story.

Student Model

Topic Sentence

Circle the topic sentence. What does Ashley tell?

Evidence

Draw a box around the text evidence. Is there any other evidence in the selection Ashley can tell about?

Concluding Statement

Underline the concluding statement. Why is it a good way to end the paragraph?

In "The Dream Catcher," the author uses what Peter and Nokomis do and say to tell a story. At the beginning, Peter is upset. Nokomis shows him a dream catcher. They make one together. Then Peter shares his culture with his class. The author uses what Peter and Nokomis say and do to tell the beginning, middle, and end of the story.

Richard Johnson

Leveled Reader

Sequence Write about "The Special Meal." How does the author use what the characters do and say to tell the events in the story?

In _____

the author _____

_____

For example, the author uses _____

_____

_____

The author also _____

_____

The author uses what the characters do and say

_____

_____

Topic Sentence

☐ Include the title of the text you read.

Evidence

☐ Tell what the characters do or say.

☐ Give examples.

Concluding Statement

☐ Restate how the author uses what the characters do and say to tell the events of the story.

Essential Question

How do people from different cultures contribute to a community?

Go Digital!

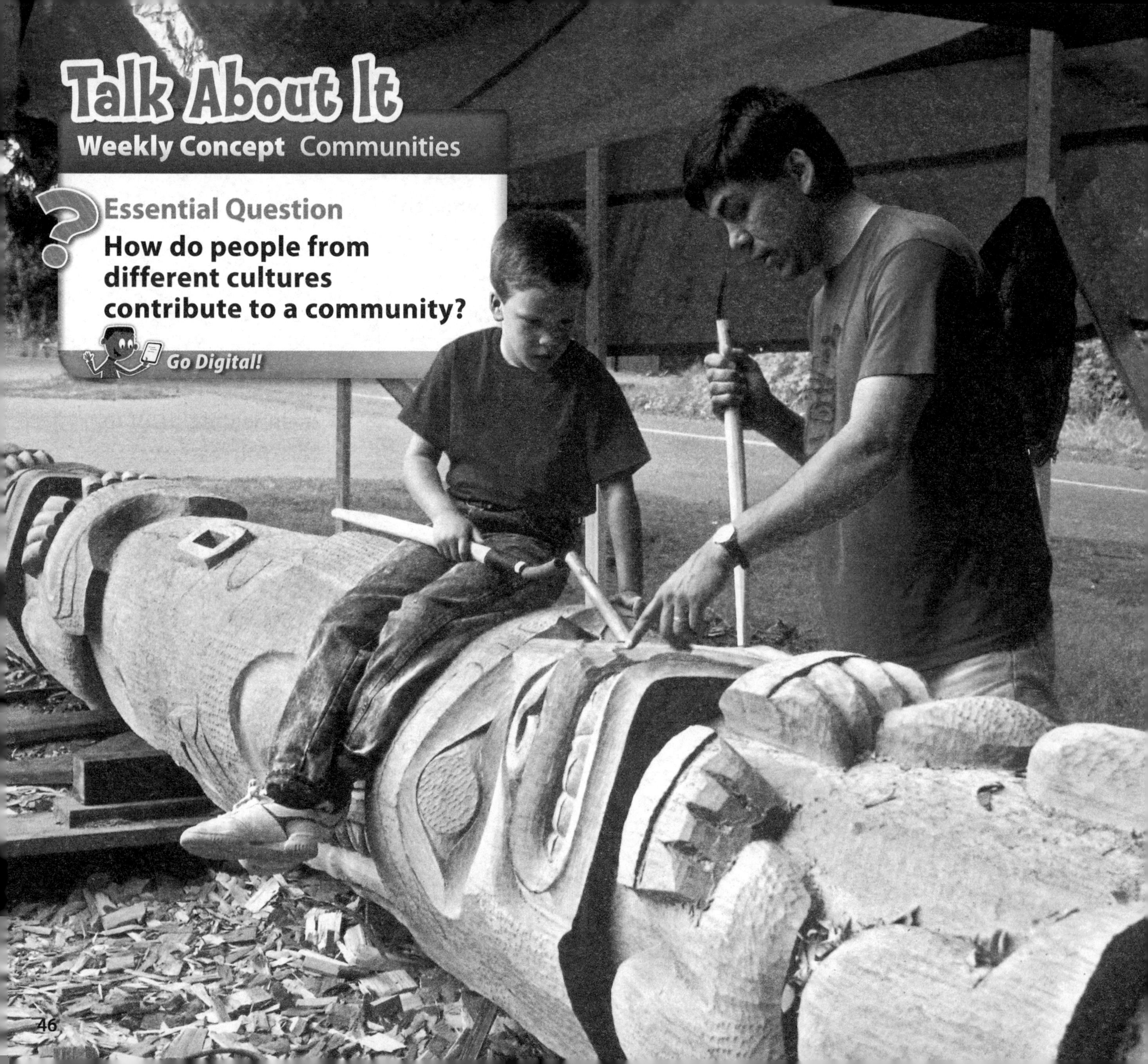

46

Write words that tell how people can share their cultures with others.

Sharing Cultures

Describe how you could share your culture. Use words from above.

Vocabulary

Work with a partner to complete each activity.

1 pronounce

Some words are easy to *pronounce*, or say. Write a word that is easy for you to *pronounce*.

Aubrey

2 scared

Mindy is *scared* of thunder. She is afraid of loud noises. What word means the same as *scared*?

frightened, afraid

3 classmate

My *classmate* and I are working together on a project. What do you and a *classmate* do together?

work

4 practicing

Kit is *practicing* her soccer skills. Why do people practice doing things?

to be better

5 contribute

Ray asked his friends to *contribute* to a food drive. Name something you might *contribute* to a food drive.

canned soup

6 tumbled

The marbles *tumbled* off the table. Read the sentence above out loud. What is another word for *tumbled*?

fall

7 **admires**

Act out how a person looks when he or she *admires*, or likes, a new bicycle.

8 **community**

Draw a picture of a member of your *community* who helps people.

High-Frequency Words

▶ **Read** each word. **Spell** each word. **Write** each word.

about ___about___

with ___with___

they ___they___

soon ___soon___

my ___my___

day ___day___

Read the story. **Circle** the high-frequency words.

Ruth wanted to do something (about) the park. There was too much trash. One (day) she went (with) a friend. (They) picked up trash. (Soon) the park was clean.

Read "Room to Grow." Use this page to take notes as you read.

_____

_____

_____

_____

_____

_____

_____

_____

_____

_____

_____

Room to Grow

Our new home in Portland

 **Essential Question**

How do people from different cultures contribute to a community?

Read how one family helps a community grow.

Spring in the City

My name is Kiku. My family moved to Portland.

Our new home did not have a yard. So Mama made an indoor garden. First she and Papa planted seeds in pots. Next they put the pots on shelves. Soon our house was full of plants.

I was **scared** to start school. Would I have friends? I was afraid. But I met a **classmate** named Jill Hernandez. Her name was hard to say. She helped me **pronounce** it. The next day we were best friends.

A map of Oregon

OREGON

PENDLETON

PORTLAND

SALEM

EUGENE

ASHLAND

KEY
• CITY
★ CAPITAL
~ RIVER

Text Evidence

❶ Connection of Ideas Ⓐ Ⓒ Ⓣ

Reread the first paragraph. Who is telling this story?

_____

Draw a box around the text evidence.

❷ Comprehension
Sequence

Reread the second paragraph. **Underline** the first thing Mama and Papa did.

❸ Comprehension
Sequence

What did Mama and Papa do next?

_____

_____

Circle the signal word.

1 Connection of Ideas (A)(C)(T)

Reread the first paragraph. Who does Jill and her mother visit?

_____

2 Expand Vocabulary

Served means gave out. Reread the second paragraph. How many steps does it take Mama to *serve* tea?

_____

3 Comprehension
Sequence

What does Mama do first when she serves tea?

_____

Underline what Mama does next.

An Idea for a Garden

One day, Jill and her mother came to visit. Jill's mother said, "Jill **admires** your garden. She tells me so much about it."

We sat down. Mama **served** tea. First she put tea in the bowl. Next she added hot water and stirred. Then she gave the bowl to Jill's mother and bowed.

Mama's tea bowl

Grandmother in Japan

"My mother taught me how to make tea," said Mama. "She also taught me how to plant a Japanese garden. They grow in small, **compact** spaces."

"Our **community** wants to plant a small garden," said Jill's mother. "Could you help?"

Mama and Papa bowed.

"Yes," they said.

Text Evidence

❶ **Expand Vocabulary**

Reread the first paragraph. **Draw a box around** a word that means almost the same as **compact**.

❷ **Connection of Ideas** Ⓐ Ⓒ Ⓣ

What country did Mama live in as a young girl?

_____

Circle the text evidence.

❸ **Comprehension** Sequence

What do Mama and Papa do when Jill's mother asks them for help?

_____

_____

Text Evidence

1 **Comprehension**
Sequence

Reread the first paragraph.
Underline what happens first.
Circle the signal word.

2 **Connection of Ideas** ACT

Look at Kiku's pictures and
read the captions. Who plants
seeds?

_____

3 **Comprehension**
Sequence

Reread the second paragraph.
What is the first thing Kiku and
Jill do after Papa builds boxes?

_____

Underline the text evidence.

A Garden Grows

First, there was a meeting. Everyone in the
community wanted to **contribute**, or give,
something. Then the next day we started.

Papa built long boxes. Jill and I filled them
with dirt. We put the tallest box in back. We
put the shortest box in front.

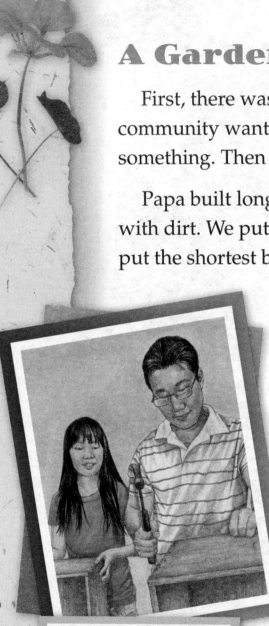

Papa builds boxes

Jill and I plant seeds

We made a rock path. Stones are **important**, or have great meaning, in Japanese gardens. Finally, we planted seeds.

We grew many vegetables. Then we picked them and had a cookout. Mama and Papa brought Japan to Portland. I was proud.

Look what we picked!

Text Evidence

1 **Expand Vocabulary**

Reread the first paragraph. What words help you figure out what **important** means?

_____

2 **Comprehension Sequence**

Reread the second paragraph. What does everyone do after they grow the vegetables?

_____

3 **Connection of Ideas** Ⓐ Ⓒ Ⓣ

How does Kiku feel about sharing her culture with her new community?

_____

Draw a box around the text evidence.

55

Respond to Reading

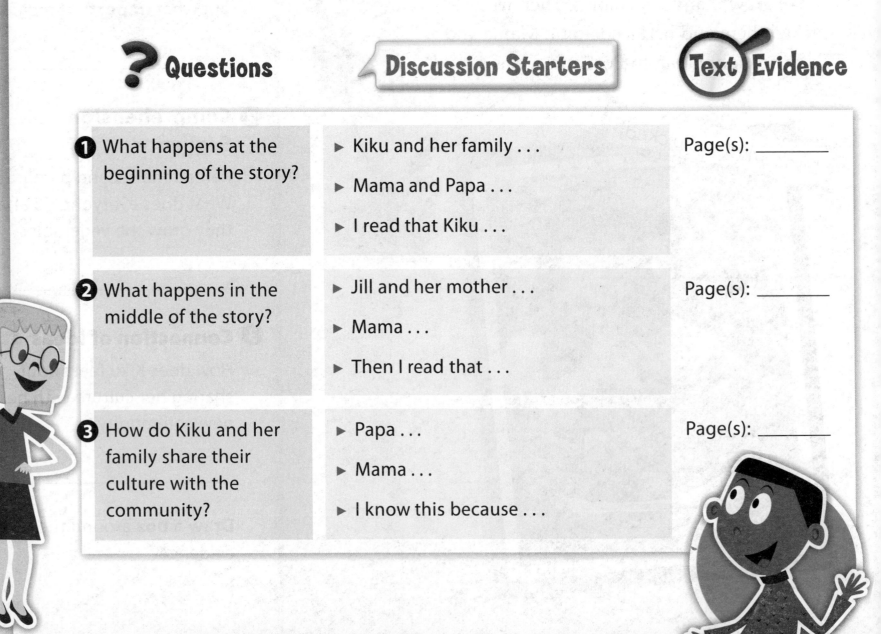

COLLABORATE

Discuss Work with a partner. Use the discussion starters to answer the questions about "Room to Grow." Write the page numbers.

? Questions

Discussion Starters

Text Evidence

1 What happens at the beginning of the story?

▶ Kiku and her family . . .

▶ Mama and Papa . . .

▶ I read that Kiku . . .

Page(s): _____

2 What happens in the middle of the story?

▶ Jill and her mother . . .

▶ Mama . . .

▶ Then I read that . . .

Page(s): _____

3 How do Kiku and her family share their culture with the community?

▶ Papa . . .

▶ Mama . . .

▶ I know this because . . .

Page(s): _____

Michael Moran

8/31/23

✏️ **Write** Review your notes. Then use text evidence to answer the question below.

How does Kiku and her family share their culture with the community?

Kiku and her family _They plant seeds._

_____

Jill's mother _wants to plant a garden for their community_

_____

Mama and Papa _they make boxes and plant seeds for Jill's community_

_____

They brought Japan to Portland by _gardens_

_____

©Japack/amanaimages RF/Corbis

Write About Reading

Shared Read

Student Model

Topic Sentence

Circle the topic sentence. What does Jay tell?

Evidence

Draw a box around the text evidence. Is there any other evidence in the selection that Jay can tell about?

Concluding Statement

Underline the concluding statement. Why is it a good way to end the paragraph?

In "Room to Grow," Kiku uses signal words to tell events in order. First, there was a meeting. Then Papa built boxes. They filled them with dirt. Next, Jill and Kiku planted seeds. Finally, they picked the vegetables and had a cookout. Kiku uses words like "first" and "finally" to tell the story events in order.

Meryl Treatner

58

Leveled Reader

In _____

the author _____

For example, the author uses _____

_____

_____

The author also _____

_____

_____

The author uses signal words _____

_____

Topic Sentence

☐ Include the title of the text you read.

Evidence

☐ Tell what signal words the author used.
☐ Give examples.

Concluding Statement

☐ Restate how the author uses signal words to put the events of the story in order.

59

Talk About It

Weekly Concept Inventions

Essential Question

How can problem solving lead to new ideas?

Go Digital!

60

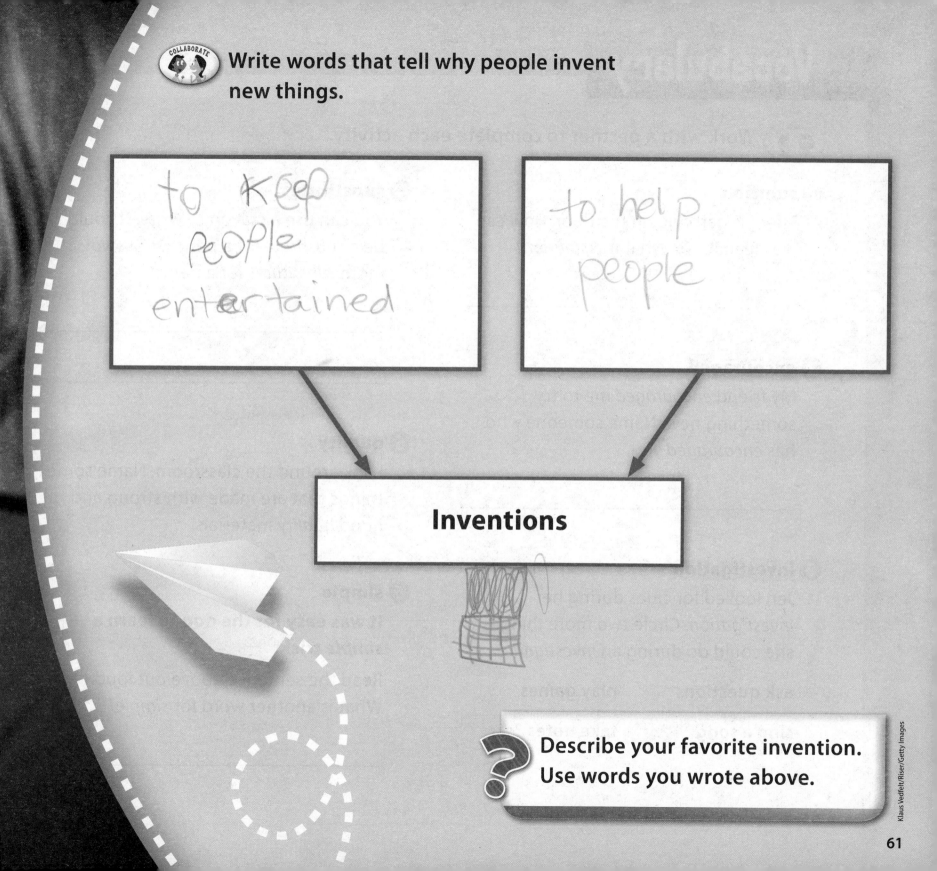

Write words that tell why people invent new things.

to keep people entertained

to help people

Inventions

Describe your favorite invention. Use words you wrote above.

Vocabulary

Work with a partner to complete each activity.

1 solution

There is garbage on the floor. How can we clean it up? What is a *solution*?

_____

2 encouraged

My friend *encouraged* me to try something new. Name someone who has *encouraged* you.

_____

3 investigation

Jen looked for clues during her *investigation*. Circle two more things she could do during an *investigation*:

ask questions	play games
sing a song	take notes

4 substitutes

You can use a crayon to write. It could be a *substitute* for a pencil. List two more *substitutes* for a pencil.

_____

_____

5 quality

Look around the classroom. Name some things that are made with strong and good *quality* materials.

6 simple

It was easy for the dog to learn a simple trick.

Read the sentence above out loud. What is another word for *simple*?

_____

7 **examine**

What does a dentist *examine*?

_____

8 **design**

Create a new backpack. *Design* one that will solve a problem. Draw it here.

▶ **Read** each word. **Spell** each word. **Write** each word.

so ___so_____

then ___then_____

because ___because_____

not ___not_____

were ___were_____

see ___see_____

Read the story. **Circle** high-frequency words.

Tom wanted a toy car. So he made one. First he drew a plan. Then he found parts. He worked hard because he wanted it to go fast. Tom's friends wanted to see it.

My Notes

Read "Mary Anderson's Great Invention." Use this page to take notes.

_____

_____

_____

_____

_____

_____

_____

_____

_____

_____

Mary Anderson's GREAT INVENTION

Essential Question

How can problem solving lead to new ideas?

Read how Mary solved a problem. She invented something new.

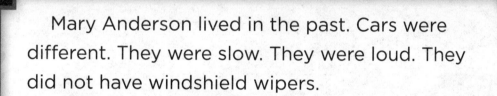

Mary Anderson lived in the past. Cars were different. They were slow. They were loud. They did not have windshield wipers.

Rain made it hard for drivers to see. So they rubbed onions on their windshields. Onions have oil. As a result, the oil kept the rain off. It would **repel** rain and snow. This was not a good **solution**. Nothing else worked. Then Mary Anderson solved the problem.

Malene Laugesen

Text Evidence

1 Connection of Ideas A C T

Why was it hard for drivers to see when it rained? **Circle** the sentence that tells why.

2 Comprehension
Cause and Effect

What happened when drivers rubbed onions on their windshields?

_____

_____

3 Expand Vocabulary

What words help you figure out what **repel** means?

_____

Draw a box around two things drivers wanted to *repel*.

65

Text Evidence

1 **Comprehension**
Cause and Effect

Why did Mary ride a streetcar?

She felt cold snow

Circle the signal word that helps you figure out the cause and effect.

2 **Expand Vocabulary**

Reread the third paragraph. What words help you know what **wiped** means? Write another word that means almost the same thing.

3 **Connection of Ideas** **ACT**

Draw a box around the last sentence. Then reread the page. Name two things Mary saw that helped her think of her idea.

It Started with Snow

Mary went to New York City in 1902. It was snowing. She rode a streetcar because she felt cold and wet.

There was snow on the windshield. The driver could not see. Mary watched the driver push open the windshield. This helped. But it was cold. Snow got into the car.

Mary saw other cars stop. Drivers got out. They **wiped** the snow off their windshields. This was a big problem. Mary had an idea.

The Next Steps

Mary **sketched** her idea. She drew a picture and made notes. She wanted to **examine**, or look at, her idea. First she looked for facts about what drivers needed.

Next, Mary made a **design**, or a plan. It looked **simple**. She hoped it would be easy to use.

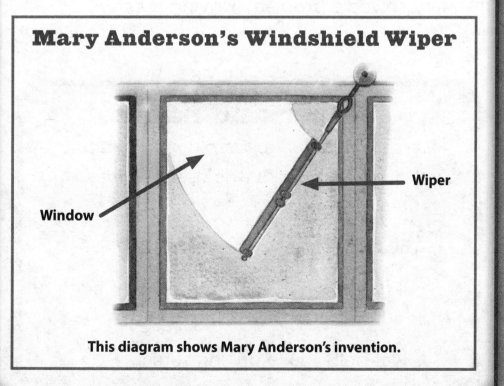

Mary Anderson's Windshield Wiper

Window

Wiper

This diagram shows Mary Anderson's invention.

Malene Laugesen

Text Evidence

1 Expand Vocabulary

What words help you figure out the meaning of **sketched**?

_____

_____

2 Comprehension
Cause and Effect

Reread the first paragraph. Why did Mary sketch her idea and make notes?

_____

_____

3 Connection of Ideas A C T

A diagram is a simple drawing with labels. Look at the diagram. **Draw a box** around two parts of Mary's invention that are labels.

Text Evidence

1 **Connection of Ideas** (A)(C)(T)

Reread the first paragraph. How did Mary test her invention?

_____

_____

2 **Comprehension**
Cause and Effect

The wiper moving back and forth is the effect. **Underline** the cause. **Circle** the signal words.

3 **Comprehension**
Cause and Effect

Reread the second paragraph. What caused driving to be safer?

_____

Draw a box around the text evidence.

Mary wanted to build a model, so she used **quality** materials. It was time to test her invention. The driver moved a handle. As a result, the wiper moved back and forth. It wiped off snow and rain. Mary's idea worked! This **encouraged** her. She was happy about her invention.

Solving the Problem

Mary solved a problem. Driving is safer because of her idea.

Better and Safer

Cars from long ago were not as safe as cars today. As a result, the seat belt was invented.

- The first seat belt was used in 1885.

- All riders in cars must wear a seat belt. It is a **law**, or rule.

- Seat belts make driving safer.

Text Evidence

❶ Comprehension

Cause and Effect

Reread the sidebar on page 68. Why was the seat belt invented? **Underline** the cause. **Circle** the signal words.

❷ Expand Vocabulary

A **law** is something we have to do. Look at the sidebar on page 68. Write another word that means almost the same as *law*.

_____

❸ Connection of Ideas Ⓐ Ⓒ Ⓣ

Reread page 68. Find one thing that windshield wipers and seat belts have in common.

Draw a box around the text evidence.

69

Respond to Reading

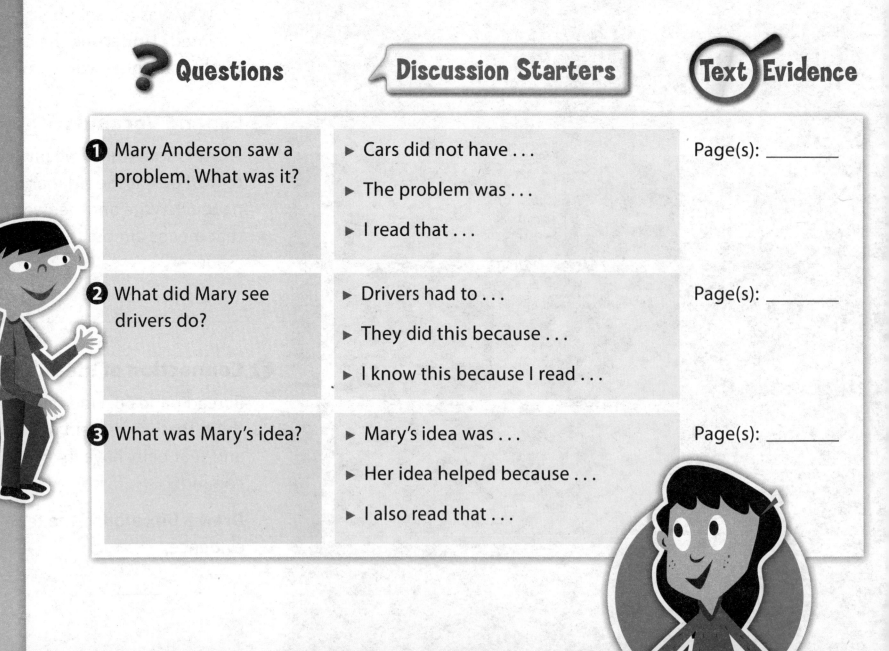

COLLABORATE

Discuss Work with a partner. Use the discussion starters to answer the questions about "Mary Anderson's Great Invention." Write the page numbers.

? Questions

Discussion Starters

Text Evidence

1 Mary Anderson saw a problem. What was it?

▸ Cars did not have . . .

▸ The problem was . . .

▸ I read that . . .

Page(s): _____

2 What did Mary see drivers do?

▸ Drivers had to . . .

▸ They did this because . . .

▸ I know this because I read . . .

Page(s): _____

3 What was Mary's idea?

▸ Mary's idea was . . .

▸ Her idea helped because . . .

▸ I also read that . . .

Page(s): _____

How did problem solving lead Mary Anderson to a new idea?

Mary saw a problem. I read that _they used onions to_
clear off windsheilds.

Then she had an idea. Mary's idea was to _make wisheld_

Then she _tested it._

Mary's idea _was good!_

Malene Laugesen

Write About Reading

Shared Read

Text Features Read Jon's paragraph about "Mary Anderson's Great Invention." He analyzed how the author uses text features to help explain the topic.

Student Model

Topic Sentence

Circle the topic sentence. What does Jon tell?

Evidence

Draw a box around the text evidence. Is there any other evidence in the selection Jon could tell about?

Concluding Statement

Underline the concluding statement. Why is it a good way to end the paragraph?

In "Mary Anderson's Great Invention," the author uses text features to help me understand the topic. For example, the diagram of Mary's invention gives me more information. It shows me what her windshield wiper looked like. It also names the parts. The author uses this text feature to teach me more about the topic.

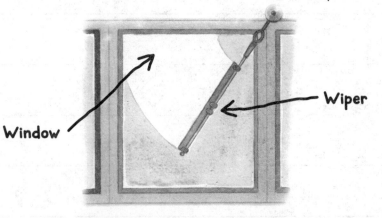

Window   Wiper

Leveled Reader

In _____,

the author _____

_____

For example, the author uses _____

_____

_____

The author also _____

_____

The author uses the text features to help me ____

_____

_____

Topic Sentence

☐ Include the title of the text you read.

Evidence

☐ Tell what text features the author used.
☐ Give examples.

Concluding Statement

☐ Tell how the text features helped you understand what you read.

73

Essential Question

How do landmarks help us understand our country's story?

Go Digital!

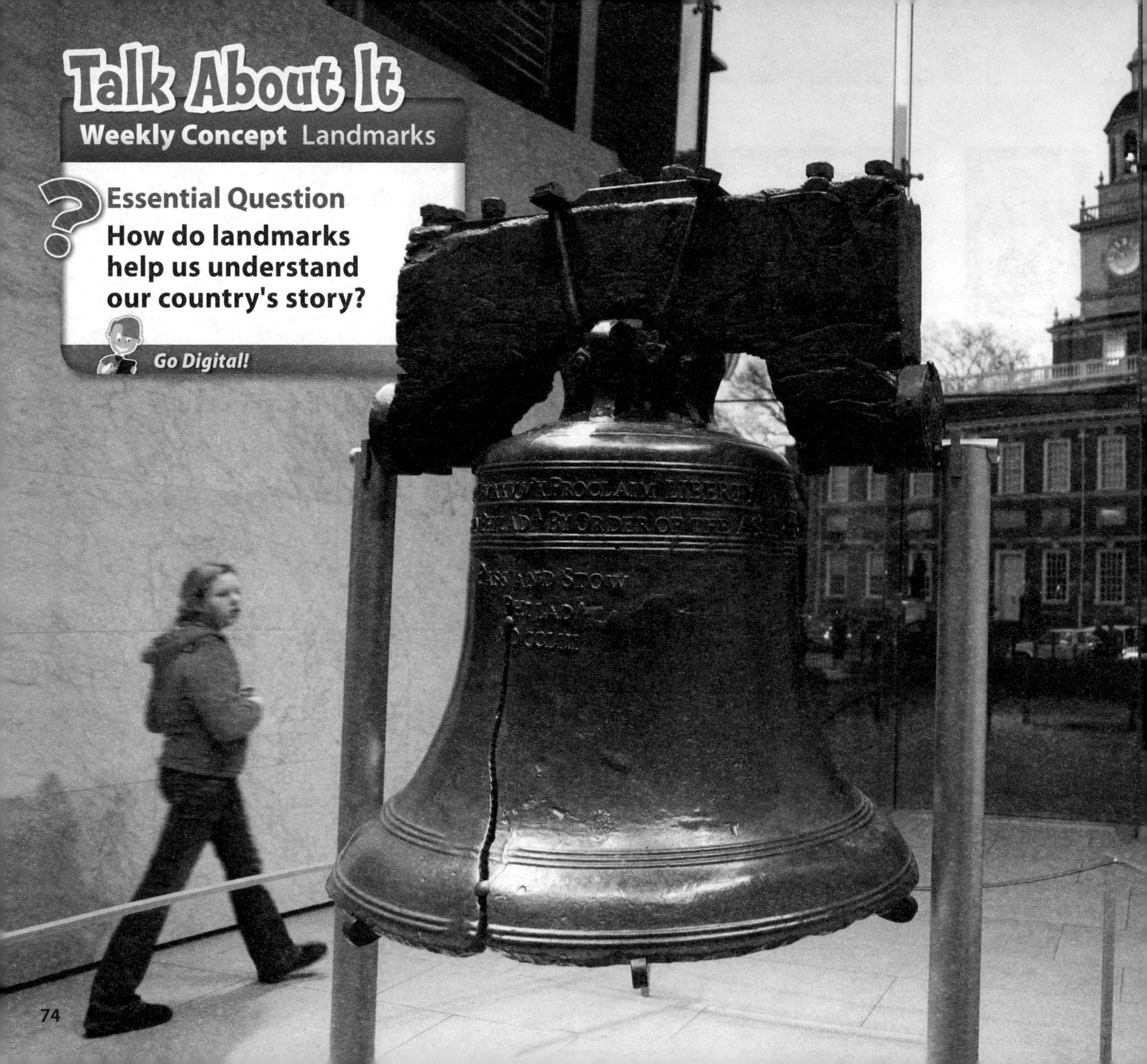

Write words that tell what people can learn by visiting landmarks.

Landmarks

 Describe a monument and what it teaches. Use words from above.

Vocabulary

Work with a partner to complete each activity.

1 traces

Lori had *traces*, or small bits, of green clay on her fingers. What words help you understand what *traces* means?

_____

2 grand

Carly thought the *grand* waterfall was huge and majestic. Name something you think is *grand*.

_____

3 carved

Noel *carved*, or cut, a dog out of a piece of wood.

Read the sentence above aloud. What is another word for *carved*?

_____

4 massive

Ann stared at the *massive* redwood tree in the forest. What makes something *massive*?

_____

5 national

Circle two *national* holidays that are celebrated in America:

Thanksgiving   **Tim's birthday**

First day of school   **Memorial Day**

6 monument

Tell about a time you visited a *monument*. Describe something you learned about history at the landmark or *monument*.

clues

List two *clues* that might help you find something.

_____

_____

 **landmark**

Draw a picture of a *landmark*.

High-Frequency Words

▶ **Read** each word. **Spell** each word. **Write** each word.

each _____

saw _____

look _____

also _____

have _____

old _____

Read the story. **Circle** high-frequency words.

Leo once (saw) the Mississippi River. They have steam boat rides. You also can look at the old boats. Each boat has its own history.

My Notes

Read "A Natural Beauty." Use this page to take notes as you read.

_____

_____

_____

_____

_____

_____

_____

_____

_____

_____

Essential Question

How do landmarks help us understand our country's story?

Read about what one national landmark teaches us.

A Natural Beauty

It is a famous **landmark** in the United States. It is **huge**! It is one mile deep. It is ten miles wide. The Colorado River **carved** it out of rock. It stretches across four states. What is it? It's the **Grand** Canyon!

Exploring the Canyon

Almost five million people visit the Grand Canyon each year. They come from all around the world. They hike the trails. They ride boats down the river. They gaze at the **massive** cliffs.

Nature lovers visit the Grand Canyon, too. They look for animals. They find many kinds of plants. They see eagles, snakes, and bats. Some visitors come to the canyon to learn about history.

Text Evidence

1 **Expand Vocabulary**

The Grand Canyon is **huge**. **Circle** the words that tell about the Grand Canyon's size.

What does *huge* mean?

_____

2 **Organization** (A)(C)(T)

What is the section "Exploring the Canyon" about?

_____

_____

3 **Comprehension**
Main Idea and Key Details

Reread the section "Exploring the Canyon." **Underline** key details that tell about why people visit the Grand Canyon.

79

Text Evidence

1 **Expand Vocabulary**

Use the details to tell what **scientists** do.

_____

_____

2 **Comprehension**

Main Idea and Key Details

Reread. **Underline** key details that tell about what scientists found. What do these key details have in common?

3 **Comprehension**

Main Idea and Key Details

Reread the key details. Use them to write the main idea.

_____

_____

_____

History of the Canyon

Native Americans were the first people to live in the Grand Canyon. One group was the Ancestral Puebloans.

The Ancient Pueblo people lived in cliff houses like these.

The Ancestral Puebloans lived in the canyon for many years. They were farmers and hunters. **Scientists** have found **traces**, or parts, of their old homes.

Scientists have found very old rocks in the canyon. These rocks are **clues**. They tell how the canyon was formed. Scientists have also found tools. Tools tell about the people who lived there.

The Grand Canyon

This map shows where the Grand Canyon is located.

UTAH

NEVADA

GRAND CANYON NATIONAL PARK

Colorado River

Lake Mead

Las Vegas

Colorado River

North Rim

Grand Canyon Village

ARIZONA

○ City
— Highway
▨ Grand Canyon National Park

Kingman

Flagstaff

It's a Landmark

President Theodore Roosevelt visited the Grand Canyon. He said it was a special place. As a result, he made it a **national monument**. Then it was **declared** a national park in 1919. The president announced that the land is protected. No one can build there. Everyone can enjoy the Grand Canyon.

Protect the Canyon

People need to care for national landmarks. They can help in many ways. Visitors can follow park rules. They can keep away from animals. They can keep the rivers clean. We can still learn a lot from this beautiful landmark. It is important to protect it.

Bighorn sheep live in the Grand Canyon.

Text Evidence

❶ Expand Vocabulary

Circle the word that helps you figure out what **declared** means.

❷ Organization ⒶⒸⓉ

Reread the first paragraph. President Roosevelt said the Grand Canyon was a special place. That's the cause. What is the effect?

_____

Draw a box around the signal words.

❸ Comprehension
Main Idea and Key Details

Reread the sidebar. **Underline** key details that tell about how people can care for landmarks.

Use the key details to tell the main idea.

Respond to Reading

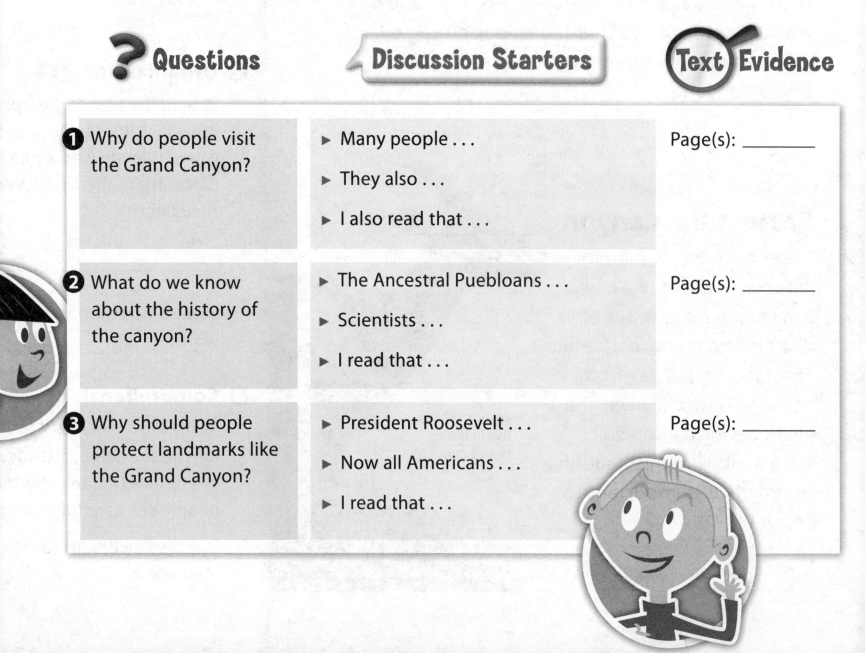

Discuss Work with a partner. Use the discussion starters to answer the questions about "A Natural Beauty." Write the page numbers.

? Questions

Discussion Starters

Text Evidence

1 Why do people visit the Grand Canyon?

▶ Many people . . .

▶ They also . . .

▶ I also read that . . .

Page(s): _____

2 What do we know about the history of the canyon?

▶ The Ancestral Puebloans . . .

▶ Scientists . . .

▶ I read that . . .

Page(s): _____

3 Why should people protect landmarks like the Grand Canyon?

▶ President Roosevelt . . .

▶ Now all Americans . . .

▶ I read that . . .

Page(s): _____

Mike Moran

82

Write Review your notes. Then use text evidence to answer the question below.

How does the Grand Canyon help us understand our country's story?

People visit the Grand Canyon to _____

_____

Scientists have learned that _____

_____

President Roosevelt _____

_____

_____

People should protect landmarks because _____

_____

_____

Write About Reading

Shared Read

Read Toni's paragraph about "A Natural Beauty." She analyzes how the author uses key details to tell the main idea.

Student Model

Topic Sentence

Circle the topic sentence. What does Toni tell?

Evidence

Draw a box around the text evidence. Is there any other evidence in the selection Toni can tell about?

Concluding Statement

Underline the concluding statement. Why is it a good way to end the paragraph?

In "A Natural Beauty," the author gives key details to tell the main idea that people visit the Grand Canyon for many reasons. The author tells that visitors hike and boat. Many people go to see animals and plants. People also visit to learn about history. The author uses these key details to tell the main idea that many people visit the canyon.

Leveled Reader

Write about "The National Mall." How does the author use key details to tell the main idea in Chapter 1?

In _____

the author uses key details to _____

_____

For example, the author says that _____

_____

_____

The author also says that _____

_____

These key details _____

_____

Topic Sentence

☐ Include the title of the text you read.

Evidence

☐ Tell how the author uses key details to support the main idea.

☐ Give examples.

Concluding Statement

☐ Restate how the author supported the main idea using key details.

Figure It Out

The Big Idea

What does it take to solve a problem?

Talk About It

?

Essential Question

Why is working together a good way to solve a problem?

Go Digital!

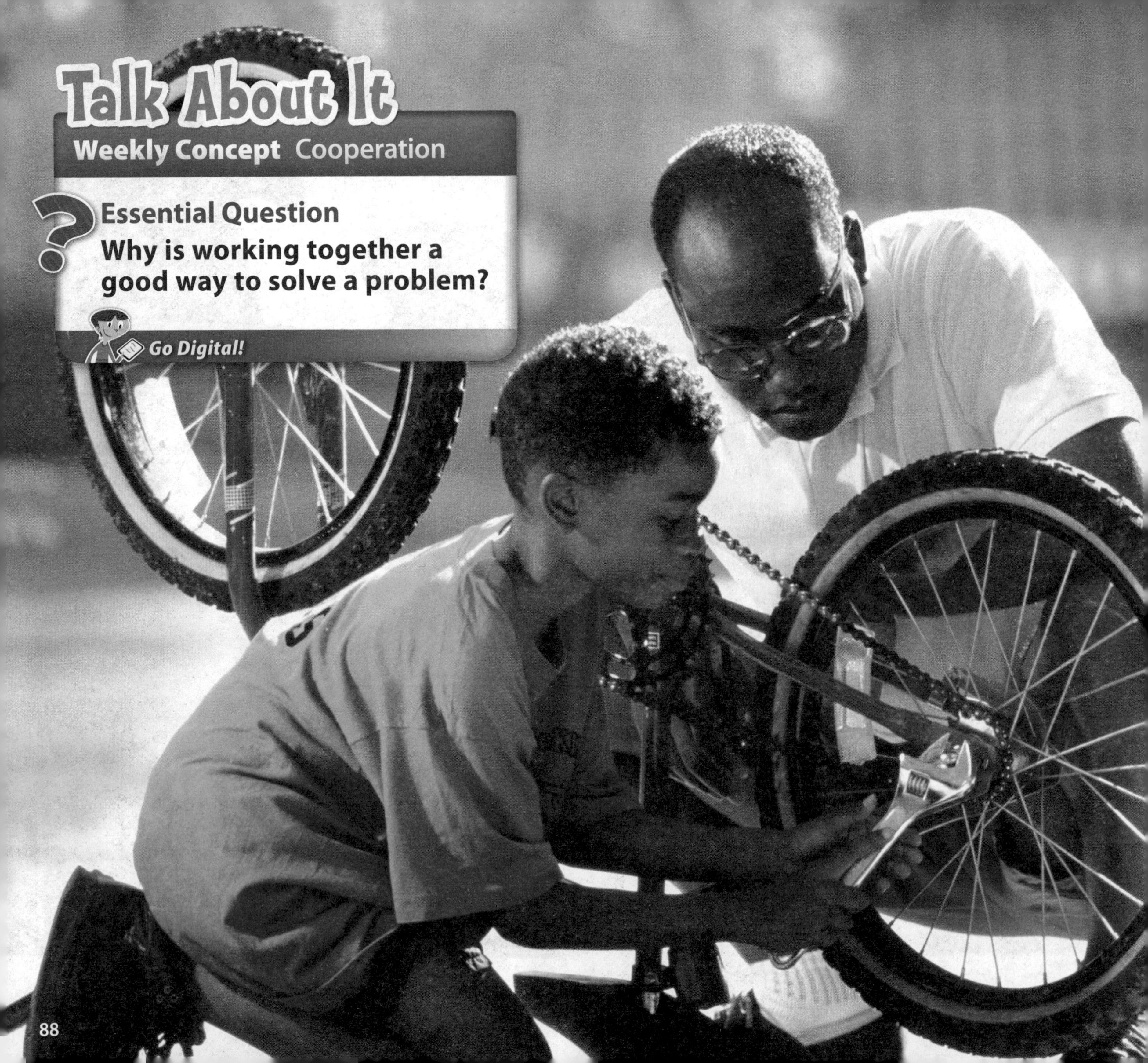

Write words that tell how working together helps solve problems.

Working Together

 Describe a time when you worked together to solve a problem.

Vocabulary

 Work with a partner to complete each activity.

1 attempt

Lou made an *attempt* to surprise his sister. Tell about an *attempt* you made to do something.

_____

_____

2 created

Will *created* a new song for his mom. Tell about something you have *created*.

_____

3 interfere

My new puppy likes to *interfere*, or get in the way, when I am reading.

Read the sentence above out loud. Write the words that tell what *interfere* means.

_____

4 awkward

Write about something you do that looks *awkward*.

_____

_____

5 cooperation

Write one thing you can do faster with a friend's *cooperation*.

_____

6 furiously

Li said no and shook his head *furiously*. Circle the words that tell what *furiously* means.

in a sleepy way   **in a quiet way**

in an angry way   **in a slow way**

7 **timid**

Hello, is anybody there?

Read the sentence above out loud in a *timid* voice. Then, read it again using a brave voice.

8 **involved**

Draw a picture of an activity or hobby you are *involved* in right now.

High-Frequency Words

▶ **Read** each word. **Spell** each word. **Write** each word.

one _____

play _____

said _____

another _____

he _____

your _____

Read the story. **Circle** high-frequency words.

"This box is too big for one boy to pick up," said Chad. So he asked Jared to help. They worked together. Then they went outside to play.

My Notes

Read "Anansi Learns a Lesson." Use this page to take notes as you read.

_____

_____

_____

_____

_____

_____

_____

_____

_____

_____

_____

Anansi
Learns a Lesson

Essential Question

Why is working together a good way to solve a problem?

Read how Turtle works with a friend to solve his problem.

Anansi the Spider always ate lunch at the same time. One day, Turtle came by.

"Those bananas look good," said Turtle. "I am hungry."

Anansi didn't want to share. He wanted to play a trick on Turtle.

"Have one," said Anansi with a **sly** grin.

Text Evidence

1 **Comprehension**
Theme

Reread page 93. **Circle** two key details that tell you about Anansi.

2 **Sentence Structure** Ⓐ Ⓒ Ⓣ

Write one thing Turtle says.

_____

_____

3 **Expand Vocabulary**

A **sly** person is not always honest and likes to play tricks on others. Why does Anansi have a *sly* grin?

_____

_____

Draw a box around the text evidence.

Text Evidence

1 Comprehension
Theme

Reread the first paragraph. What does Anansi do while Turtle washes his hands?

_____

Circle the sentence that supports your answer.

2 Comprehension
Theme

Reread the third paragraph. What does Anansi do after Turtle washes his hands?

_____

3 Sentence Structure A C T

Reread the last sentence aloud. What does Anansi think about what he did to Turtle?

_____

"You should wash your hands," said Anansi. So Turtle did. When he got back, Anansi had eaten half of the bananas.

Turtle made another **attempt** to eat. But Anansi said, "Please wash your hands."

Turtle was too shy and **timid** to say no. When he got back, the bananas were gone.

Anansi laughed. "I tricked you!"

Turtle was angry. He wanted to teach Anansi a lesson.

"Come to my house for dinner," he said.

Anansi said yes. Turtle asked Fish for help.

"With your **cooperation**, we can trick Anansi," said Turtle. So the friends **created** a **clever** plan.

Text Evidence

1 Sentence Structure Ⓐ Ⓒ Ⓣ

Draw a box around what Turtle tells Anansi to do. What does Anansi say?

_____

2 Comprehension
Theme

Reread the third paragraph. Why does Turtle ask Fish for help?

_____

_____

3 Expand Vocabulary

The word **clever** means smart. Why does the plan need to be _clever_?

_____

_____

Text Evidence

❶ Comprehension

Theme

Reread the third paragraph. What details tell why Anansi can't get to Turtle's house?

_____

_____

_____

Circle the text evidence.

❷ Expand Vocabulary

Reread the fourth paragraph. **Draw a box** around a word that helps you understand what **sank** means.

❸ Sentence Structure Ⓐ Ⓒ Ⓣ

Reread the last paragraph. **Underline** the command.

The next day, Turtle and Fish went to the lake. Anansi was there.

"Let's swim to Turtle's house," said Fish.

Anasi was a clumsy and **awkward** swimmer. He was also too light. He couldn't swim down to the bottom of the lake.

"Hold some big stones," said Fish. So Anansi picked up two stones. He **sank** down to Turtle's house.

"Welcome, Anansi," said Turtle. "Drop those stones and eat."

Anansi dropped the stones. He **rocketed** to the surface of the lake. He was angry and gasped **furiously**.

"They tricked me," he said.

Turtle and Fish laughed.

"We worked together and taught Anansi a lesson," said Turtle.

"We also solved a problem," said Fish. "Let's eat!"

Text Evidence

❶ Expand Vocabulary

Reread the second paragraph. **Underline** the root word in **rocketed**. Does it mean to move slowly or quickly?

_____

❷ Comprehension
Theme

How did Turtle and Fish trick Anansi?

Circle the details that tell how.

❸ Comprehension
Theme

What is the theme or message of this story?

_____

Draw a box around the text evidence.

Respond to Reading

COLLABORATE

Discuss Work with a partner. Use the discussion starters to answer the questions about "Anansi Learns a Lesson." Write the page numbers.

? **Questions**

Discussion Starters

Text Evidence

1 How does Anansi trick Turtle?

▶ Anansi . . .

▶ He tricks Turtle by . . .

▶ Then I read that . . .

Page(s): _____

2 What does Turtle want to do?

▶ Turtle wants to . . .

▶ He asks Fish . . .

▶ Then I read that . . .

Page(s): _____

3 How do Turtle and Fish work together?

▶ Turtle and Fish . . .

▶ Fish tells Anansi to . . .

▶ They work together to . . .

Page(s): _____

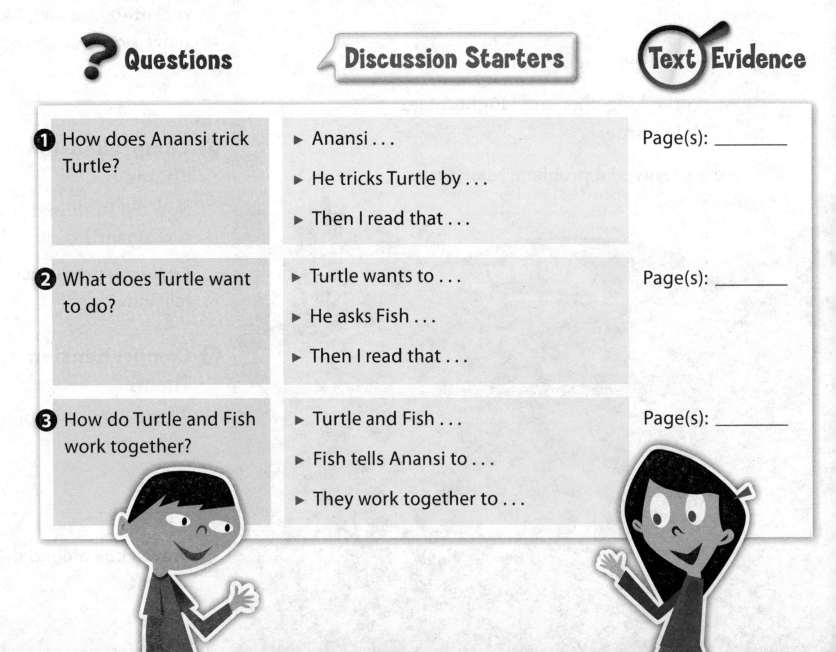

Write Review your notes. Then use text evidence to answer the question below.

How do Turtle and Fish work together to teach Anansi a lesson?

Anansi _____

_____

Turtle asks Fish to _____

_____

_____

Turtle and Fish _____

_____

They teach Anansi a lesson by _____

_____

_____

Janet Broxon

Write About Reading

Shared Read

Read an Analysis **Theme** Read Sasha's paragraph below about "Anansi Learns a Lesson." She analyzes how the author uses what the characters do and say to share the theme.

Student Model

Topic Sentence

Circle the topic sentence. What does Sasha tell?

Evidence

Draw a box around the text evidence. Is there any other evidence in the story Sasha can tell about?

Concluding Statement

Underline the concluding statement. Why is it a good way to end the paragraph?

In "Anansi Learns a Lesson," the author uses what Fish and Turtle do and say to tell about the theme of working together. In the beginning of the story, Anansi tricks Turtle. Turtle is angry. He asks Fish to help him. They work together to trick Anansi. The author uses what Fish and Turtle do and say to share the theme that working together helps solve problems.

Leveled Reader

Theme Write about "The Quarreling Quails." How does the author use what the characters do and say to share the theme?

In _____

the author _____

_____

For example, the author uses _____

_____

The author also _____

_____

The author uses what the characters do and say

to _____

_____

_____

Topic Sentence

☐ Include the title of the text you read.

Evidence

☐ Tell how the author uses what the characters do and say to tell the theme.

☐ Give examples.

Concluding Statement

☐ Restate how the author uses what the characters do and say to show the theme, or message.

Talk About It

Weekly Concept Immigration

Essential Question

Why do people immigrate to new places?

Go Digital!

102

Write words that tell about why people immigrate, or move, to new places.

Immigration

 Tell about why people move to new places. Use words you wrote above.

Vocabulary

 Work with a partner to complete each activity.

1 opportunity

An art show is a good *opportunity*, or chance, to show off your skills. What word helps you understand *opportunity*?

_____

2 moment

Greg stood in the rain for a *moment* before running inside. Name something that lasts for a *moment*.

_____

3 arrived

Penny *arrived* home on the school bus. List one way you can *arrive* somewhere.

_____

4 immigrated

People *immigrated* to the United States for many reasons. Read the list of words below aloud. Circle two words that mean almost the same as *immigrated*.

traveled   quit   arrived   saw

5 valuable

The time I spend with my grandma is *valuable*. Name something that is *valuable* to you.

_____

6 photographs

We emailed *photographs* from our trip to our grandparents. Tell your partner one way that *photographs* and drawings are different.

7 **whispered**

Amber *whispered* to Jake in the middle of class. Quietly *whisper* what your favorite color is to your partner.

8 **inspected**

Think of something you have *inspected*. Draw a picture of what you might use to *inspect* something.

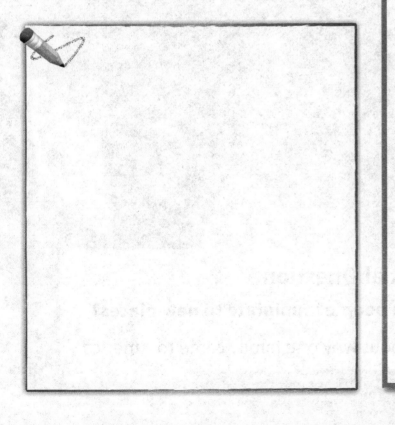

High-Frequency Words

▶ **Read** each word. **Spell** each word. **Write** each word.

she _____

know _____

find _____

down _____

want _____

all _____

Read the story. **Circle** the high-frequency words.

Beth's family moved. (She) didn't want to go. She was sad to leave all of her friends. "You will find new friends," said Mom. Beth said, "I know."

My Notes

Read "Sailing to America." Use this page to take notes as you read.

_____

_____

_____

_____

_____

_____

_____

_____

_____

_____

_____

SAILING TO AMERICA

Essential Question

Why do people immigrate to new places?

Read about why one family came to America.

Tristan Elwell

Nora couldn't sleep. It was March, 1895. Da was leaving for America today. Uncle Sean had **immigrated** there last year and found work. He asked Da to come. It was Mama and Da's dream to live in America.

Nora lit a lamp and sat at the table. Her brother, Danny, joined her.

"I feel like crying," he **whispered** softly.

"I know," said Nora. "So do I. But this is Da and Mama's dream. Da will find work. Then we can go there, too."

❶ **Comprehension**
Theme

What was Mama and Da's dream?

_____

_____

Underline the text evidence.

❷ **Genre** ⒶⒸⓉ

Use the illustration. **Circle** two clues that show this story is historical fiction.

❸ **Genre** ⒶⒸⓉ

Reread the page. What two clues show that this story takes place a long time ago?

_____

_____

107

1 Comprehension
Theme

Reread the first paragraph. **Underline** the reason why Danny doesn't want to leave Ireland and go to America.

2 Expand Vocabulary

If you have **enough**, you have all that you need. Write another word for *enough*.

_____

3 Comprehension
Theme

Reread the second paragraph. What does Nora tell Danny about moving to America?

_____

_____

Underline the text evidence.

"I don't want to leave Ireland," said Danny. "We won't have any friends in America."

"Maybe you will like it there," Nora said. "We will have **enough** food to eat. We'll all have a better life. America will be the land of our dreams."

Tristan Elwell

108

A year later, Da had enough money. He sent for Mama, Danny, and Nora. They packed and got on a **crowded** ship full of people.

The voyage across the ocean was hard. The ship tossed up and down. The waves were very big. Many people got sick on the trip.

Every day Nora reread Da's letters. She dreamed of his big smile.

Text Evidence

1 Expand Vocabulary

Reread the first paragraph. What words help you figure out what **crowded** means?

_____

2 Genre Ⓐ Ⓒ Ⓣ

How was traveling across the ocean hard? **Circle** the details that tell about Nora and her family's trip.

3 Comprehension
Theme

Reread the third paragraph. How do you know that Nora misses Da?

_____

_____

Underline the text evidence.

Text Evidence

1 Genre ACT

Compare the picture on page 109 with the picture on this page. Describe the clues that show the trip took a long time.

2 Comprehension
Theme

Reread the first paragraph. What did Nora notice when she woke up?

_____

Underline the text evidence.

3 Genre ACT

How did the immigrants know they had arrived in America?

_____

_____

One morning Nora awoke. In a **moment** she knew something was different. The ocean was still.

"There's Lady Liberty!" someone shouted. "We've **arrived** in America!"

The **travelers** went to Ellis Island. Doctors **inspected** them. Mama answered questions. They only had one **opportunity**, or chance. They had to pass.

Finally the family learned they could stay in America. They got off the boat. Nora saw Da waving and smiling. Dreams do come true, she thought.

Tristan Elwell

Text Evidence

1 Expand Vocabulary

Who are the **travelers** in this story?

_____

_____

2 Genre ACT

Reread the first paragraph. **Circle** two things Nora and her family did at Ellis Island.

3 Comprehension
Theme

Reread the third paragraph. Describe what Nora saw when she got off the boat.

What is the theme of this story?

_____

_____

Underline the text evidence.

Respond to Reading

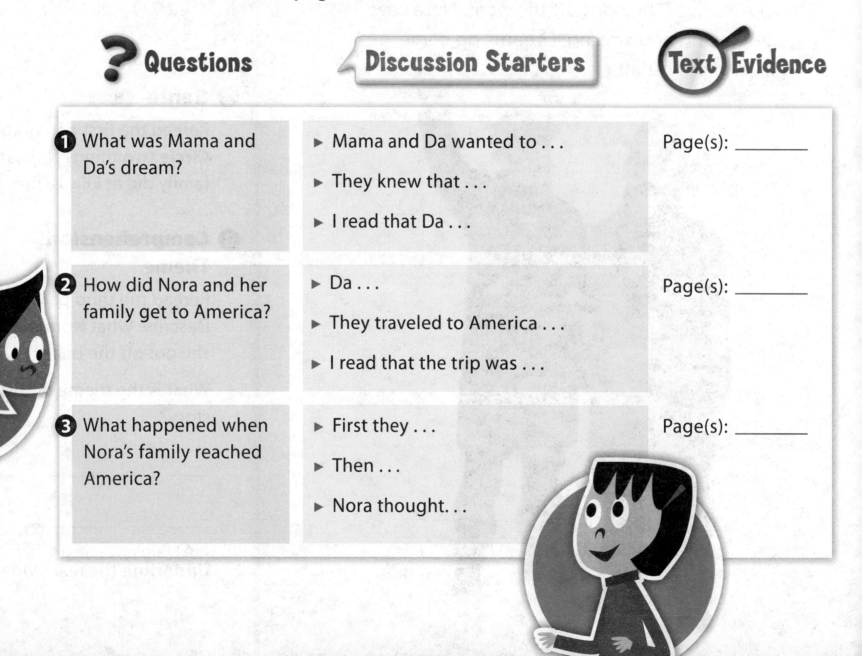

COLLABORATE

Discuss Work with a partner. Use the discussion starters to answer the questions about "Sailing to America." Write the page numbers.

? Questions

Discussion Starters

Text Evidence

1 What was Mama and Da's dream?

- ▶ Mama and Da wanted to . . .
- ▶ They knew that . . .
- ▶ I read that Da . . .

Page(s): _____

2 How did Nora and her family get to America?

- ▶ Da . . .
- ▶ They traveled to America . . .
- ▶ I read that the trip was . . .

Page(s): _____

3 What happened when Nora's family reached America?

- ▶ First they . . .
- ▶ Then . . .
- ▶ Nora thought. . .

Page(s): _____

Write Review your notes. Then use text evidence to answer the question below.

Why did Nora and Danny's family immigrate to America?

Da went to America to find _Work._

Then, the family _got on the boat._

When they got to America, they _were checked by doctors._

Nora thought that _dreams do come true._

Write About Reading

Shared Read

Student Model

In "Sailing to America," the author uses what Nora says and does to share the theme. Mama and Da dream of a better life in America. First Da goes. Then, Nora, Danny, and Mama get on a boat. The trip is hard. When Nora sees her Da, she thinks dreams do come true. The author uses enough details about what Nora says and does to help me understand the theme that dreams can come true.

Topic Sentence

Circle the topic sentence. What does Ana tell?

Evidence

Draw a box around the text evidence. Is there any other evidence in the story Ana can tell about?

Concluding Statement

Underline the concluding statement. Why is it a good way to end the paragraph?

Tristan Elwell

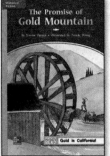

Leveled Reader

Write an Analysis ▸ **Theme** Write about "The Promise of Gold Mountain." Do you think the author uses enough details about what the characters do and say to show the theme in Chapter 1?

In _____

I think the author _____

_____

For example, the author shows _____

_____

The author also shows _____

_____

The author uses what the characters feel and do

to _____

_____

Topic Sentence
☐ Include the title of the text you read.

Evidence
☐ Tell how the author uses theme to help readers understand the story.
☐ Give examples.

Concluding Statement
☐ Restate how the author uses what the characters do and feel to show the theme, or message.

116

Write words that tell how you can let other people know what you think.

Government

 Name ways to let people know what you think. Use words you wrote.

Vocabulary

 Work with a partner to complete each activity.

1 announced

The judge *announced* the winner at the end of the race. Act out how the judge might have *announced* it.

2 government

People vote for *government* leaders. Name a *government* leader.

_____

3 elect

We vote to *elect*, or choose, people to lead our country. Write two synonyms for *elect*.

_____

_____

4 independent

Justin makes his own lunch and that helps him feel more *independent*. What does it mean to be *independent*?

_____

5 convince

Emily tried to *convince* her friend to go to the park.

Read the sentence above out loud. Act out what Emily might say to her friend to *convince* her to go to the park.

6 estimate

Look around the classroom. Without counting, *estimate*, or guess, how many books you see. What word means almost the same as *estimate*?

_____

7 candidates

What if there were three *candidates* for class president. Tell your partner how you would decide who to vote for.

8 decisions

We make lots of *decisions* every day. Draw two foods you might decide to have for breakfast.

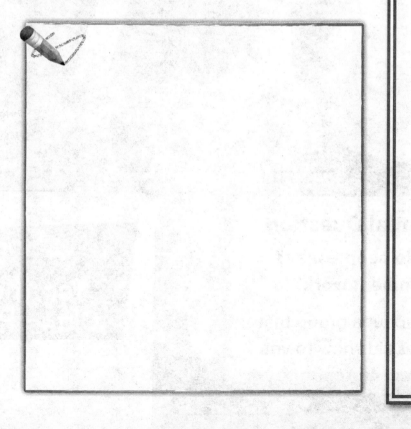

High-Frequency Words

▶ **Read** each word. **Spell** each word. **Write** each word.

how _____

who _____

new _____

is _____

people _____

only _____

Read the story. **Circle** the high-frequency words.

Two (people) want to be the new president. There can be only one. Today is voting day. How will you vote? Who will win?

VOTE

My Notes

Read "Every Vote Counts!"
Use this page to take notes
as you read.

_____

_____

_____

_____

_____

_____

_____

_____

_____

_____

Every VOTE Counts!

Essential Question

How do people make government work?

Read about a group that teaches kids how to vote.

Vote for the Class Pet

Have you ever voted? Did you vote for a class pet? Voting is important. It tells people what you think.

Many years ago, our leaders wrote a plan for our **government**. The plan gave people the right to vote.

People pick leaders. They vote on new laws. Voting gives them the **power** to choose.

Text Evidence

1 Comprehension
Author's Point of View

Reread the first paragraph. What details tell what the author thinks about voting?

_____

Circle the text evidence.

2 Organization ACT

Reread the second paragraph. What words tell you that the details happened in the past?

_____

3 Expand Vocabulary

Reread the third paragraph. What **power** does voting give people?

_____

Underline the text evidence.

Text Evidence

1 Comprehension
Author's Point of View

Reread the first paragraph. What does the author think about why people don't vote? **Circle** the words that tell you what the author thinks.

2 Comprehension
Author's Point of View

What does the author think about Kids Voting USA?

_____

Circle the text evidence.

3 Organization A C T

Reread the second paragraph. When kids learn to vote, what do they do first?

_____

Underline the signal word.

Teaching Kids to Vote

Many people don't vote. They think it's too hard. They think it takes too long. That's sad. Kids Voting USA hopes to **convince** more people to vote. That's good!

Kids Voting USA teaches kids about voting. They give teachers lessons to use. First, kids read stories. They learn how to **elect**, or choose, a good leader.

It is Election Day!

First we sign in.

Next, kids talk about voting at home. They read about **candidates**. Candidates are the people who want to be leaders. Kids talk and make **decisions**. They decide who they will vote for.

Kids vote on **election** day. They use **ballots**. A ballot has the names of candidates on it. Kids mark their choices. Then they put their ballot into a box. The votes are counted. Finally the winners are **announced**. Everyone knows who won.

Then we mark a ballot.

Finally we vote!

BALLOT BOX

Text Evidence

❶ Expand Vocabulary

Reread the second paragraph. What do kids do on **election** day?

_____

❷ Expand Vocabulary

What are **ballots** for?

_____

Underline the text evidence.

❸ Organization ⒶⒸⓉ

Look at the photos at the bottom of the page. What do kids do on Election Day?

First _____

Then _____

Finally _____

Text Evidence

1 Comprehension
Author's Point of View

Reread the first paragraph. Why does Kids Voting USA want kids to vote now?

Circle the sentences that answer the question.

2 Organization A C T

Reread the second paragraph. What three things will you be able to do someday?

3 Comprehension
Author's Point of View

Circle the sentence that tells what the author thinks about kids voting someday. Write the author's point of view here.

Vote Now

Voting gives kids the power to share how they feel. Kids Voting USA wants kids to vote now. They think this will help. They think when kids grow up, more will vote.

Someday you will be able to vote. You will have the power to help elect great leaders. You can help make new laws. That's exciting!

Kids can learn to vote at school.

This bar graph shows the results of a class election. Which pet won?

Vote for a class Pet

Hamster
Hermit Crab
Guinea Pig
Mouse

0 1 2 3 4 5 6 7 8

Everyone in this class voted. Isn't that great?

Phil Coale/AP Images

Text Evidence

❶ Organization Ⓐ Ⓒ Ⓣ

What pets did the class vote on?

_____

_____

❷ Organization Ⓐ Ⓒ Ⓣ

Look at the bar graph. Which animal got the most votes?

_____

❸ Comprehension
Author's Point of View

Look back at the text evidence you circled.

What is the author's point of view about voting?

_____

_____

125

Respond to Reading

COLLABORATE

Discuss Work with a partner. Use the discussion starters to answer the questions about "Every Vote Counts!" Write the page numbers.

? Questions | **Discussion Starters** | **Text Evidence**

---

1 Why is voting important?

▸ Voting is important because . . .

▸ When people vote, they . . .

▸ I read that . . .

Page(s): _____

---

2 How does Kids Voting USA teach kids to vote?

▸ Kids learn to vote by . . .

▸ On election day . . .

▸ I know this because . . .

Page(s): _____

---

3 Why should kids learn to vote?

▸ Kids Voting USA . . .

▸ Voting . . .

▸ The author thinks voting is . . .

Page(s): _____

Write Review your notes about "Every Vote Counts!" Then write your answer to the question below. Use text evidence to support your answer.

BALLOT BOX

How do people make government work?

Voting is important because _____

_____

_____

Kids learn to vote by _____

_____

On election day, kids _____

_____

_____

When kids grow up, they will _____

_____

Write About Reading

Shared Read

Read an Analysis **Author's Point of View** Read Mario's paragraph about "Every Vote Counts!" He analyzes how the author uses details to support his point of view.

Topic Sentence

Circle the topic sentence. What does Mario tell?

Evidence

Draw a box around the text evidence. Is there any other evidence in the selection Mario can tell about?

Concluding Statement

Underline the concluding statement. Why is it a good way to end the paragraph?

Student Model

In "Every Vote Counts!" the author uses details to show what he thinks about voting. The author says that voting is important. I read that many people don't vote. The author thinks that's sad. The author also thinks that Kids Voting USA is helping. The author uses details that show that he thinks voting is important.

Leveled Reader

Write an Analysis **Author's Point of View** Write a paragraph about "The Race for the Presidency." How does the author use details to support her point of view?

In _____

the author thinks _____

_____

For example, the author says that _____

_____

_____

The author also says that _____

_____

These details support _____

_____

Topic Sentence

☐ Include the title of the text you read.

Evidence

☐ Tell how the author uses point of view.

☐ Give examples.

Concluding Statement

☐ Restate how the author supported point of view with details.

129

Essential Question

How can people help animals survive?

Go Digital!

COLLABORATE Write words that tell what animals need to survive.

Survival

? Describe how to take care of an animal. Use words you wrote above.

Vocabulary

 Work with a partner to complete each activity.

1 population

Name a *population* of animals that live near your house.

_____

2 threatened

Lia's cat felt *threatened*, or in danger, when a big dog ran into her yard.

Read the sentence above out loud. What words help you understand what *threatened* means?

_____

3 caretakers

What do *caretakers* do?

_____

_____

4 success

Bill and Ryan's lemonade stand was a big *success*. Tell about a *success* that you have had.

5 resources

People need *resources* like water and food to be healthy. Circle the *resources* that help keep us healthy.

fruit   candy

fresh air   vegetables

6 recognized

I *recognized*, or saw, my favorite baseball player. What word means the same as *recognized*?

_____

7 **survive**

Plants need many things to *survive*. Add one more thing plants need to *survive*.

dirt, sunlight, _____

8 **relatives**

We all have *relatives* or people that are our family. Draw a picture of one of your *relatives*.

High-Frequency Words

▶ **Read** each word. **Spell** each word. **Write** each word.

there _____

to _____

be _____

more _____

what _____

would _____

Read the story. **Circle** the high-frequency words.

Max asked Ted, "(What) would you do to help the fish in the pond?" Ted said, "There is trash in the pond. I would clean it up. Then add more fish."

My Notes

Read "Kids to the Rescue!" Use this page to take notes as you read.

_____

_____

_____

_____

_____

_____

_____

_____

_____

_____

KIDS to the Rescue!

Olivia and Carter started a group to help animals.

Essential Question

How can people help animals survive?

Read how two kids helped sea turtles survive an oil spill.

What a mess! There was thick, **gooey** oil everywhere. It slid across the water. It stuck to rocks and sand. The oil spill in the Gulf of Mexico was making animals sick.

Two kids from a small town watched the news. They wanted to help.

Text Evidence

❶ Comprehension
Author's Point of View

Reread the first paragraph. Which sentence tells what the author thinks about the oil spill? **Circle** it.

❷ Expand Vocabulary

Gooey means sticky and wet. **Underline** the words that help you understand the meaning of *gooey* in the first paragraph.

❸ Connection of Ideas A C T

Who did the kids want to help?

_____

Draw a box around the text evidence that supports your answer.

135

Text Evidence

1 Comprehension

Author's Point of View

What does the author think about Olivia and Carter's message?

_____

Circle the text evidence.

2 Expand Vocabulary

Reread the second paragraph. **Draw a box** around the word that helps you understand what **habitat** means.

3 Connection of Ideas ACT

What might happen to the sea turtle population if they lost their homes?

_____

Underline the text evidence.

Olivia and Carter to the Rescue!

Olivia and Carter Ries want all animals to be around for a long time. They started a group. They have a great message. They say everyone can help animals.

The kids watched the oil spill get bigger. More animals got sick. The Kemp's ridley turtle was one of them. The **population**, or number, of sea turtles was getting smaller. The oil **threatened** their homes. It was harming their **habitat**.

Olivia and Carter learned about Kemp's ridley turtles.

This turtle is clean and healthy.

Oil Spoils Everything

The oil was destroying **resources** the turtles need to live. Thick oil made it hard for them to swim.

The harmful oil spoiled their food, too. The turtles can't **survive** without food. Many would die.

(l) One More Generation; (r) Steven Senne/AP Images

1 Comprehension
Author's Point of View

Reread the heading. What does the author think about the oil spill?

_____

2 Comprehension
Author's Point of View

Reread the second paragraph. **Circle** the word that helps you figure out what the author thinks about the oil.

3 Connection of Ideas A C T

Reread both paragraphs. What was the oil destroying?

_____

_____

Circle the text evidence.

1 Expand Vocabulary

What **donations** did Olivia and Carter collect and bring to New Orleans?

_____

2 Comprehension
Author's Point of View

Reread the second paragraph. What does the author think about Olivia and Carter's plan?

_____

Circle the text evidence.

3 Connection of Ideas ACT

Look at the map. Write one new thing you learned about Olivia and Carter.

_____

Saving the Sea Turtles

Olivia and Carter **recognized** the problem. They saw that the turtles needed help. They made a plan. The kids called a rescue group. The group needed soap and wipes. So the kids asked people to help.

Olivia and Carter worked for four months. Then they went to New Orleans. Their **donations** helped people clean many turtles. Their plan worked. It was a **success**!

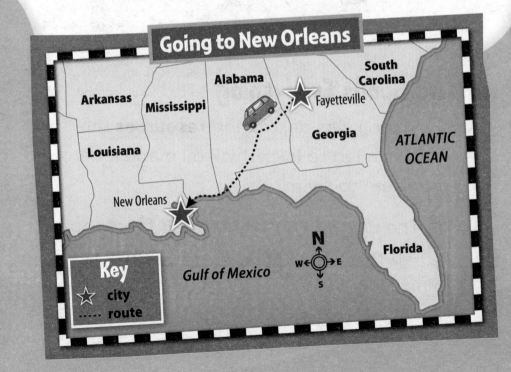

Going to New Orleans

Key
☆ city
····· route

TSI Graphics

Keeping Busy

Olivia and Carter go to schools. They tell kids everyone can save animals. They also ask leaders to make new laws that help animals. They help rescue animals in danger.

Olivia and Carter are super heroes to animals.

Carter and his mom unpack donations.

You Can Help Animals, too!

- Protect nests.
- Keep parks clean.
- Keep water clean.
- Stop using plastic bags.

Text Evidence

1 Comprehension
Author's Point of View

Reread the second paragraph. What does the author think of Olivia and Carter?

_____

Circle the text evidence.

2 Connection of Ideas 🅐🅒🅣
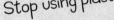

Look at the sidebar. List one way you can help animals.

_____

3 Comprehension
Author's Point of View

Look back and reread the details you circled. What is the author's point of view?

_____

_____

139

Respond to Reading

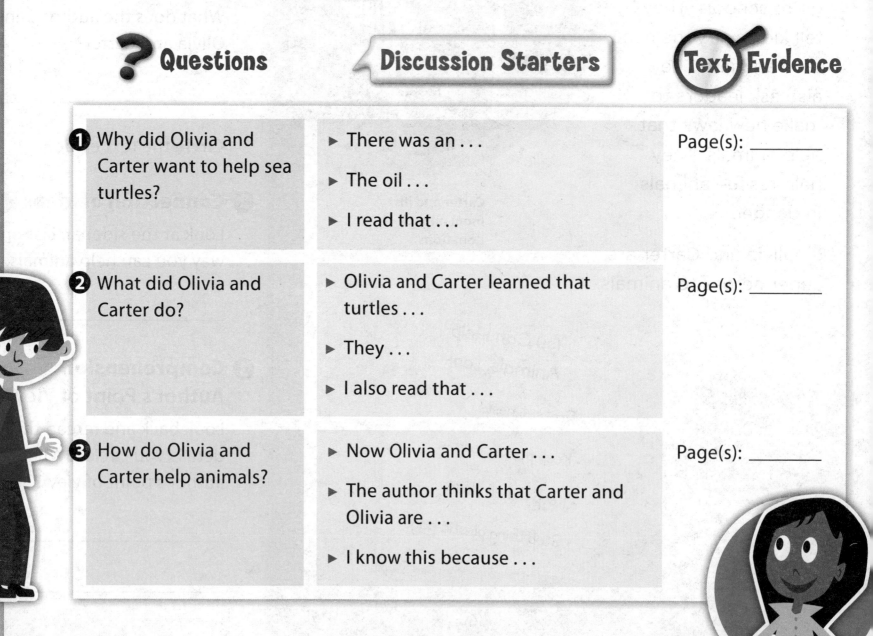

COLLABORATE

Discuss Work with a partner. Use the discussion starters to answer the questions about "Kids to the Rescue!" Write the page numbers.

❓ Questions

Discussion Starters

Text Evidence

① Why did Olivia and Carter want to help sea turtles?

▶ There was an . . .

▶ The oil . . .

▶ I read that . . .

Page(s): _____

② What did Olivia and Carter do?

▶ Olivia and Carter learned that turtles . . .

▶ They . . .

▶ I also read that . . .

Page(s): _____

③ How do Olivia and Carter help animals?

▶ Now Olivia and Carter . . .

▶ The author thinks that Carter and Olivia are . . .

▶ I know this because . . .

Page(s): _____

Mike Moran

140

Write Review your notes. Then use text evidence to answer the question below.

How do Olivia and Carter help animals survive?

Olivia and Carter _____

_____

They had a plan to _____

_____

They _____

_____

_____

Olivia and Carter are heroes to animals because _____

_____

_____

Write About Reading

Shared Read

Read an Analysis **Author's Point of View** Read Ray's paragraph about "Kids to the Rescue!" He analyzes how well the author uses details to support her point of view.

Student Model

Topic Sentence

Circle the topic sentence. What does Ray tell?

Evidence

Draw a box around the text evidence. Is there any other evidence in the selection Ray can tell about?

Concluding Statement

Underline the concluding statement. Why is it a good way to end the paragraph?

In "Kids to the Rescue!" the author uses lots of details to show that she thinks Olivia and Carter are super heroes to animals. Olivia and Carter saw news about an oil spill. They wanted to help. The author says their plan was a success. She says they are super heroes to animals. The author uses lots of details to support her point of view that helping animals is important.

Steven Senne/AP Images

Leveled Reader

Write an Analysis **Author's Point of View** Write about "Protecting the Islands." How does the author support her point of view with details? Do you agree with the author's point of view?

In _____

the author _____

For example, the author says that _____

_____

The author also says _____

_____

The author uses _____

_____

I think that _____

_____

Topic Sentence

☐ Include the title of the text you read.

Evidence

☐ Tell how the author uses point of view.

☐ Give examples.

Concluding Statement

☐ Restate how the author supported their point of view with details and tell if you agree with the point of view.

143

Talk About It

Essential Question

How do people figure things out?

Go Digital!

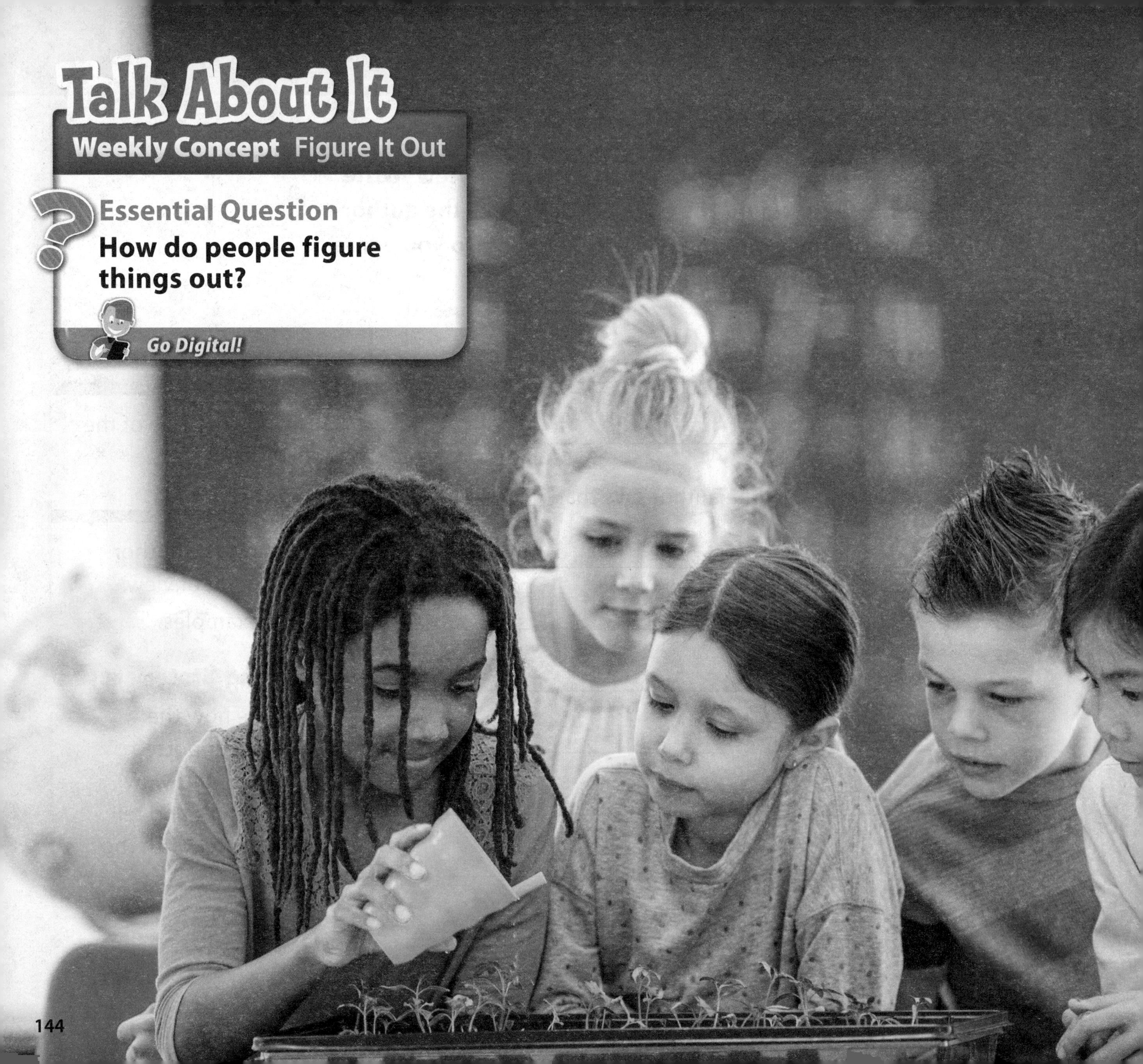

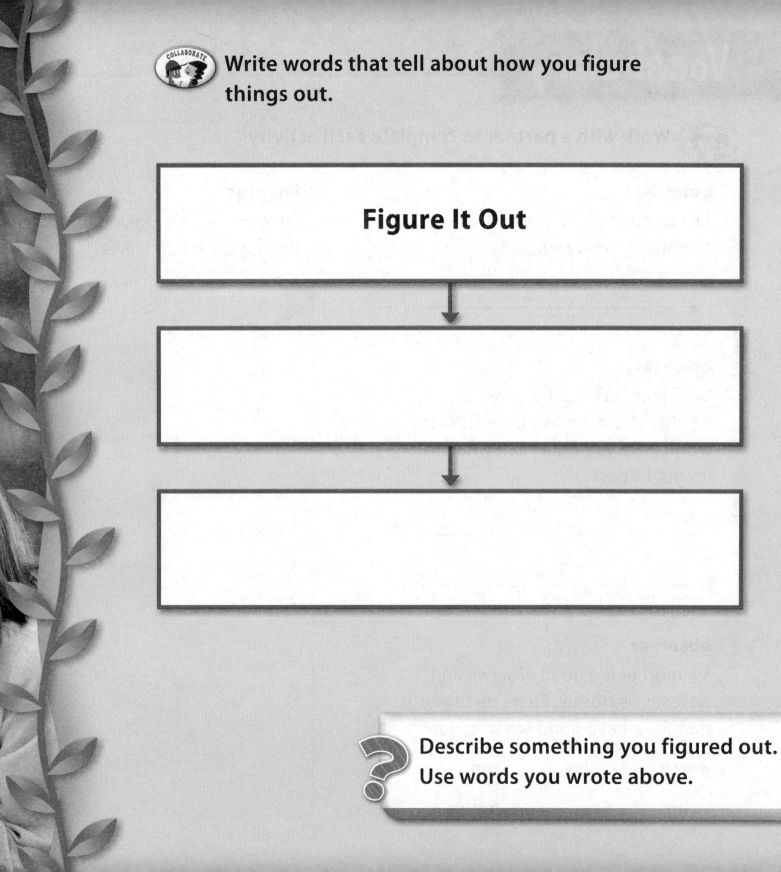

Write words that tell about how you figure things out.

Figure It Out

Describe something you figured out. Use words you wrote above.

Vocabulary

Work with a partner to complete each activity.

1 bounce

Jill can *bounce* a basketball. Name something you can *bounce*.

_____

2 inventor

Mike is an *inventor* because he likes to create new things. What words help you figure out what an *inventor* does?

_____

_____

3 observer

My mother is a good *observer* and watches us closely. Circle three words that tell what a good *observer* does.

watch   play   run

swim   see   notice

4 imagine

Imagine you are looking up at a cloud. Draw what it looks likes.

Read each poem. Work with a partner to complete each activity.

Knitting for Grandma

I tried to knit a blanket
to keep Grandma's lap warm.

My first failed try was funny.
After ten tries, it was better.

It is far from perfect,
but she loves to lay it on her lap.

Books

We wanted to know all about,
How Grandpa learned stuff without,
The help of a screen,
Or a glowing machine.
Did he read when the power went out?

5 **free verse**

Free verse poems don't have to rhyme.
Which poem is *free verse*?

_____

6 **alliteration**

Circle an example of *alliteration* in
"Knitting for Grandma."

7 **limerick**

"Books!" is a *limerick*. How many lines
does a *limerick* have?

_____

8 **rhyme**

Reread "Books!" Write another word that
rhymes with *screen*.

_____

McGraw-Hill Education

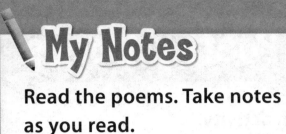

My Notes

Read the poems. Take notes as you read.

_____

_____

_____

_____

_____

_____

_____

_____

_____

_____

_____

_____

Empanada Day

One bite of Abuelita's empanadas
And my mouth purrs like a cat.
  "Teach me," I beg and bounce on my feet,
  "Teach me to make this magical treat."
Abuelita smiles,
  "Be an observer, watch and learn,
  Then you too can take a turn."

Essential Question

How do people figure things out?

Read poems about different ways to figure things out.

Dara Goldman

148

She sets before me a ball of dough,
Round and golden as the sun.
My eyes wide as saucers, I watch and follow,
   Press circles flat as pancakes,
   Spoon on apple slices and nose-tickling spices,
   Seal it all in, a half-moon envelope of bliss.
Together we write down every step
As the empanadas bake crisp in the oven,
My stomach rumbling like a hungry bear.
          Ah, empanada day!

                —George Santiago

1 Literary Elements
Alliteration

Reread the first four lines on page 148 aloud. **Circle** the words that show alliteration.

2 Comprehension
Point of View

Underline details that tell what the narrator thinks about Abuelita's empanadas.

What does the narrator think about making empanadas?

_____

_____

Underline the text evidence.

3 Connection of Ideas A C T

Circle details that help you picture what empanadas are.

Text Evidence

1 Literary Elements
Rhyme

Reread "Cold Feet." **Underline** words that rhyme with ice.

2 Connection of Ideas ⒶⒸⓉ

In "Cold Feet," what does the poet compare the inventor's toes to?

_____

3 Literary Elements
Limerick

Reread "Our Washing Machine." Write the words that rhyme.

_____

_____

_____

Cold Feet

An inventor with feet like ice
And toes like ten shivering mice,
Looked at clothes, studied feet.
Read about cold and heat,
And knit the first socks, warm and nice.

OUR WASHING MACHINE

Our washing machine is a bear
That munches up socks by the pair.
He will suds them and grumble
As they spin, turn, and tumble,
Then spit them out, ready to wear.

Dara Goldman

150

Bugged

A creature has crawled on my knee,
It's a bug green and round as a pea.
His five wings are fish fins,
He's got teeth sharp as pins.
Just imagine him chomping on me!

I read every bug book I see,
To learn what this creature might be.
I ask scientists too,
But they don't have a clue.
So I'm bugged by this great mystery.

Text Evidence

1 Literary Elements
Alliteration

Reread the poem. **Circle** words that show alliteration. Write your favorite one here.

_____

2 Comprehension
Point of View

What details tell what the narrator thinks about the bug?

_____

Underline the text evidence.

3 Connection of Ideas ⒶⒸⓉ

Reread the poem. Find examples of similes and read them aloud.

Respond to Reading

COLLABORATE **Discuss** Work with a partner. Use the discussion starters to answer the questions about "Empanada Day." Write the page numbers.

? Questions	Discussion Starters	Text Evidence
1 What happens at the beginning of the poem?	▶ The narrator . . . ▶ Abuelita . . . ▶ I read that she . . .	Page(s): _____
2 How does Abuelita make empanadas?	▶ First she . . . ▶ Then . . . ▶ Finally . . .	Page(s): _____
3 What does the narrator think about empanadas?	▶ He says . . . ▶ He . . . ▶ I know this because . . .	Page(s): _____

Write Review your notes. Then use text evidence to answer the question below.

How does the narrator figure things out?

The narrator _____

_____

Abuelita _____

_____

She makes _____

_____

_____

He watches her and _____

_____

_____

Write About Reading

Shared Read

Read an Analysis **Point of View** Read Reggie's paragraph about the poem "Our Washing Machine." He analyzes how the poet uses details to support the narrator's point of view.

Student Model

Topic Sentence

Circle the topic sentence. What does Reggie tell?

Evidence

Draw a box around the text evidence. Is there any other evidence Reggie can tell about?

Concluding Statement

Underline the concluding statement. Why is it a good way to end the paragraph?

> In "Our Washing Machine," the poet uses details to show what the narrator thinks. First I read that the narrator compares a washing machine to a bear. The poet describes what the machine does to socks. I read that it munches them up and spits them out. The poet uses details to show that the narrator thinks the washing machine is noisy.

Leveled Reader

"Problem Solved." How does the author use details to
support the narrator's point of view in Chapter 1?

In _____

the author's point of view is _____

_____

_____

For example, the author says that _____

_____

The author also says that _____

_____

These details support _____

_____

_____

Topic Sentence

☐ Include the title of the
text you read.

Evidence

☐ Tell how the author
uses details to
support the narrator's
point of view.

☐ Give examples.

Concluding Statement

☐ Restate how the
author supports point
of view using details.

Unit 3

One of a Kind

THE BIG IDEA

Why are individual qualities important?

Talk About It

Weekly Concept Be Unique

Essential Question
What makes different animals unique?

Go Digital!

158

Write words that tell about one animal's unique features.

Unique

 Describe how one animal uses its unique features to survive.

Vocabulary

 Work with a partner to complete each activity.

1 disbelief

My mother looked at the mess in *disbelief* and amazement. Circle two synonyms for *disbelief*.

wonder   sadness   surprise   fear

2 watchful

The dog kept a *watchful* eye on her new puppies. Underline the suffix. Circle the root word. What does *watchful* mean?

_____

3 dismay

Tia felt *dismay* when her best friend moved to another town.

Read the sentence above out loud. What is another word for *dismay*?

_____

4 fabulous

Sarah said the movie was *fabulous*, but James thought it was awful. Draw boxes around two words that mean the opposite of *fabulous*.

great   awful   terrible   amazing

5 offered

Ken *offered* Jody a healthy snack after the soccer game. Name a healthy snack someone has *offered* you.

_____

6 features

Animals have *features* that help them protect themselves. Name an animal and one of its *features*. Tell how the feature helps keep the animal safe.

7 **splendid**

Emma did a *splendid* job feeding her cat. What can you do in a *splendid* way?

_____

8 **unique**

Draw something that makes you *unique*.

▶ **Read** each word. **Spell** each word. **Write** each word.

by _____

carry _____

could _____

up _____

way _____

we _____

Read the story. **Circle** the high-frequency words.

There is a well (by) the tree. We put a pail in. Then we pull it up all the way. We could carry water to the cows.

John Wallner/McGraw-Hill Education

161

Read "Inchworm's Tale." Use this page to take notes as you read.

INCHWORM'S TALE

Essential Question

What makes different animals unique?

Read about how one animal helps to solve a problem.

Long ago, Anant and his sister, Anika, went swimming. They became **exhausted**. They were so tired, they climbed onto a big, flat rock and fell asleep.

As they slept, the rock beneath them grew up to the clouds.

"Sister, wake up!" Anant cried in **disbelief**. "Am I dreaming?"

"No," said Anika. "The rock grew while we slept!" They looked around and saw a **fabulous** sky and wonderful clouds.

The children could not find a way to climb down and were scared.

Text Evidence

1 Expand Vocabulary

Reread the first paragraph. What words help you figure out what **exhausted** means?

_____

_____

2 Organization ACT

Why don't Anant and Anika wake up when the rock grew?

_____

_____

3 Comprehension
Problem and Solution

Reread the page. What is Anant and Anika's problem?

_____

_____

Circle the text evidence.

Jago Silver

Text Evidence

1 **Comprehension**
Problem and Solution

What does Isha do to help solve the problem?

_____

_____

Circle the text evidence.

2 **Expand Vocabulary**

Reread the third paragraph. **Underline** the reason Hawk **squinted** his eyes. What does *squinting* help him do?

_____

3 **Comprehension**
Problem and Solution

Reread the last paragraph. **Circle** what Hawk does after he finds the children.

The villagers were worried. Isha, the village chief, saw Hawk.

"Hawk, you have **watchful** eyes and strong wings. They are your best **features**," Isha said. "Please help us."

Hawk flew into the sky. He **squinted** his eyes because the sun was so bright. Then he spotted the children.

"Don't be afraid," said Hawk. "We will save you."

Hawk could not carry the children. So he brought food and leaves.

Hawk flew down and spoke to Isha. Isha called the animals for help. Someone needed to climb the tall rock.

Mouse had strong teeth. They were **unique**, but she couldn't climb.

Bear had huge claws good for climbing trees, but they could not help him **scale** rocks.

Mountain Lion had powerful claws, but the rock was too slippery.

Finally, a tiny voice **offered** to help. "May I try? It's me, Too-Tock, the Inchworm."

Jago Silver

Text Evidence

① Comprehension
Problem and Solution

Reread the first paragraph. What does Isha do to help solve the children's problem?

_____

Circle the text evidence.

② Expand Vocabulary

Reread the third paragraph. **Draw a box** around the word that helps you figure out what **scale** means.

③ Organization Ⓐ Ⓒ Ⓣ

Which animals try to climb?

_____

_____

Underline the animal who offers to help.

165

Text Evidence

1 Expand Vocabulary

What words help you figure out what **volunteered** means?

_____

_____

2 Comprehension
Problem and Solution

Reread the page. **Circle** the sentence that tells what Hawk and Inchworm do to help solve Anant and Anika's problem.

3 Organization ACT

Reread the second paragraph. When does Inchworm make a plan for the trip down?

_____

_____

_____

Inchworm was good at climbing. Hawk **volunteered**, or said he could help, to carry Inchworm to the top of the rock.

So Hawk picked up Inchworm and they flew to the children. On the way, Inchworm made a plan for the trip down.

It took almost a week for Inchworm to lead the children down. Hawk brought them food. He also brought news to the villagers.

Finally, they reached the bottom. Inchworm was a hero!

Jago Silver

❶ Comprehension
Problem and Solution

What does Inchworm do to help the children?

_____

Circle the text evidence.

❷ Organization ＡＣＴ

Why does Hawk bring the children food?

_____

Underline the text evidence.

❸ Comprehension
Problem and Solution

Reread the story. Read aloud the steps to solve Anant and Anika's problem. In the end, who solves the problem?

_____

167

Respond to Reading

Discuss Work with a partner. Use the discussion starters to answer the questions about "Inchworm's Tale." Write the page numbers.

❓ Questions	Discussion Starters	🔍 Text Evidence
❶ What happens at the beginning of the story?	▸ Anant and Anika . . . ▸ The rock . . . ▸ The children . . .	Page(s): _____
❷ What steps do Isha and Hawk take to solve the problem?	▸ Isha asks Hawk . . . ▸ Next Isha . . . ▸ Then I read that . . .	Page(s): _____
❸ How do Hawk and Inchworm solve Anant and Anika's problem?	▸ Hawk . . . ▸ Inchworm . . . ▸ I read that . . .	Page(s): _____

Write Review your notes. Then use text evidence to answer the question below.

How do Hawk and Inchworm use their unique features to solve a problem?

First, Anant and Anika are _____

_____

_____

Next Isha asks Hawk _____

_____

Then Inchworm _____

_____

_____

Hawk and Inchworm solve the problem by _____

_____

Write About Reading

Shared Read

Read an Analysis Problem and Solution Read Naomi's paragraph about "Inchworm's Tale." She analyzes how the author uses steps Hawk and Inchworm take to solve a problem.

Student Model

In "Inchworm's Tale," the author uses what Hawk and Inchworm do to show how they solve a problem. At the beginning, Anant and Anika are stuck on a big rock. They cannot get down. Isha asks Hawk for help. Then Hawk carries Inchworm to the top of the rock. Inchworm leads the children down. The author uses the steps Hawk and Inchworm take to show how they solve Anant and Anika's problem.

Topic Sentence

Circle the topic sentence. What does Naomi tell?

Evidence

Draw a box around the text evidence. Is there other evidence Naomi could tell about?

Concluding Statement

Underline the concluding statement. Why is it a good way to end the paragraph?

Leveled Reader

Write an Analysis **Problem and Solution** Write about "The Ballgame Between the Birds and the Animals." How does the author use steps to show problem and solution in Chapter 2?

In _____

the author uses the steps the characters take to

show _____

For example, the author says _____

_____

The author also _____

_____

The author uses the steps the characters take to

_____

_____

Topic Sentence

☐ Include the title of the text you read.

Evidence

☐ Tell how the author uses steps to solving problems.
☐ Give examples.

Concluding Statement

☐ Restate how the author uses the steps to solving a problem.

Talk About It

? Essential Question

How can one person change the way you think?

Go Digital!

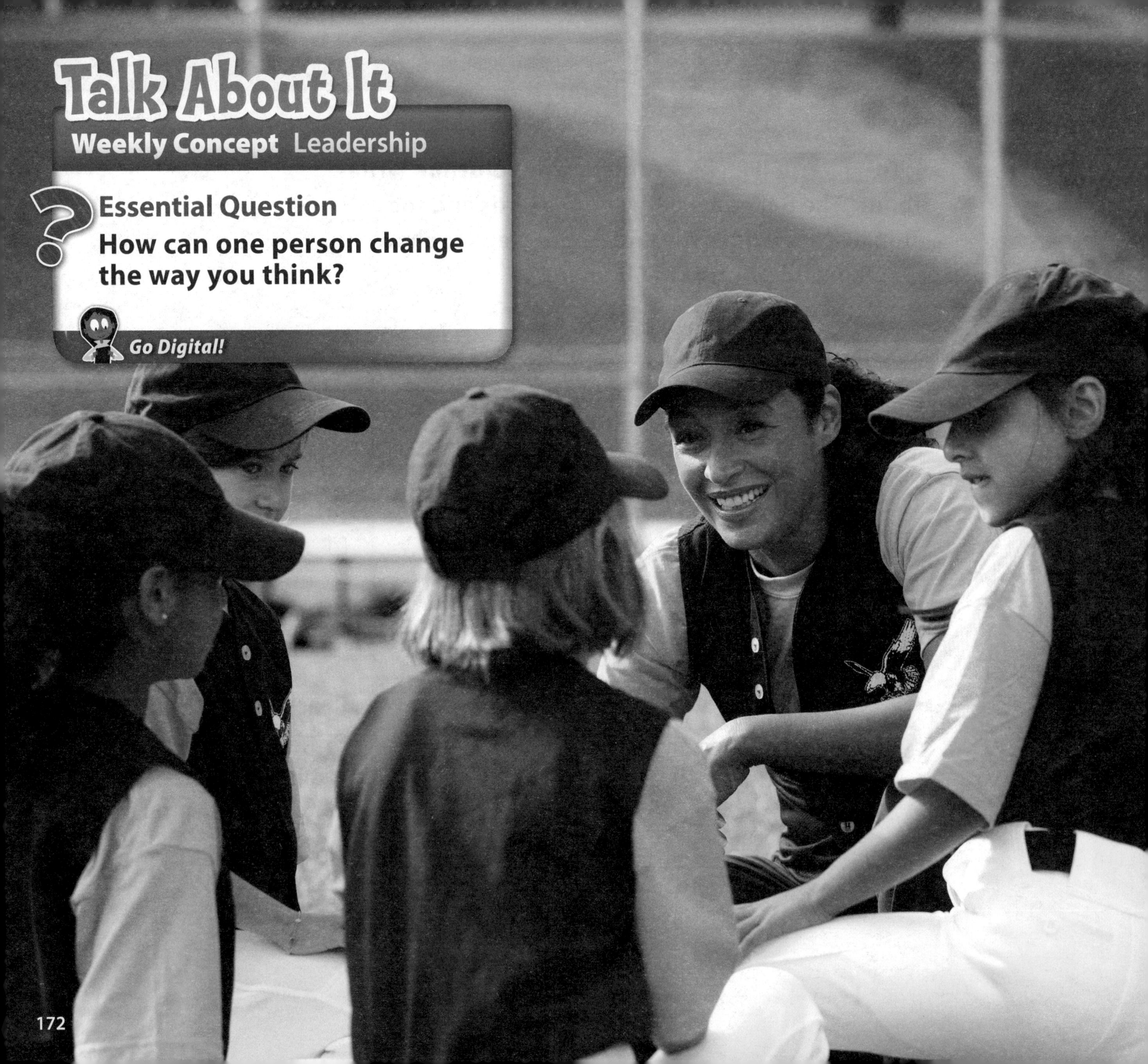

COLLABORATE Write words that describe a strong leader.

Strong Leader

? Describe a strong leader you know. Use words you wrote above.

LWA/The Image Bank/Getty Images

173

Vocabulary

 Work with a partner to complete each activity.

1 donated

Kim's class *donated* clothes to help people. Write something else that can be *donated*.

_____

2 leader

Wendy is a good *leader* because she is brave and fair. Write two more words that describe a good *leader*.

_____

_____

3 disappear

Max watched the airplane *disappear* out of sight. What words help you understand what *disappear* means?

_____

4 bravery

Name something that takes *bravery*, or courage, to do. Explain why.

5 temporary

The snow is *temporary*. Circle the words that explain why snow is *temporary*.

it will melt   **it will last forever**

it will never melt   **it will go away**

6 refused

George *refused* to help me pick up the trash. What is something you have *refused* to do?

_____

_____

_____

7 **amazement**

Jake looked at the colorful hot air balloon with *amazement*. Act out how to show *amazement*.

8 **nervous**

Draw a picture of an animal you would feel *nervous* standing close to.

High-Frequency Words

▶ **Read** each word. **Spell** each word. **Write** each word.

are _____

many _____

me _____

no _____

of _____

year _____

Read the story. **Circle** high-frequency words.

Lisa told (me) that many animals have no place to live. People are cutting down trees. I am worried that next year, more animals will not have homes.

My Notes

Read "Jane's Discovery." Use this page to take notes as you read.

_____

_____

_____

_____

_____

_____

_____

_____

_____

_____

Jane's Discovery

? Essential Question

How can one person change the way you think?

Read how a future president changed Jane's life.

Peter Ferguson

Jane slammed the door of her cabin and raced toward the woods. Her parents **insisted** that she go to school. They told her she had to learn to read. It was September of 1825, and Jane wanted to help on the farm like her brothers. Therefore, she told her parents, "No!" She **refused**.

Jane splashed through a stream. She ran and ran. She ran around a tree and wasn't paying attention. As a result, she tripped over Abe Lincoln's legs.

Abe was reading. He smiled and helped Jane up.

Text Evidence

❶ **Expand Vocabulary**

Reread the first paragraph. **Circle** words that help you figure out **insisted**.

❷ **Organization** Ⓐ Ⓒ Ⓣ

What does Jane do after her parents insist she go to school and learn to read?

_____

❸ **Comprehension**
Cause and Effect

Reread the second paragraph. What happens when Jane isn't paying attention?

_____

_____

Underline the signal words.

Text Evidence

1 Expand Vocabulary

What does **upset** mean? **Draw a box** around a word that means almost the same.

2 Comprehension
Cause and Effect

Why is Jane running?

_____

_____

_____

Circle the signal word.

3 Comprehension
Cause and Effect

Reread the last paragraph. Why is Jane worried and upset?

Underline the cause.

"Why are you running?" Abe asked.

"I'm running because I'm worried and **upset**," said Jane. "My parents want me to learn to read and I told them no!"

Peter Ferguson

"Reading can change your life," said Abe. "I'll show you."

The next day, Abe showed Jane a book about George Washington. He had read it many times.

Abe read aloud to Jane. He read that Washington was a great leader. He read about Washington's courage and **bravery**.

"I want to be like George Washington," said Abe. "Someday I will be **president**, too."

"You will make a great president, because you're a great leader now," said Jane. "You changed my mind about reading."

Abe smiled. "Tell your parents you will learn to read," he said. "I will help you."

Text Evidence

1 Organization (A)(C)(T)

Reread the second paragraph. **Draw a box** around the words that tell you when the event takes place.

2 Expand Vocabulary

Reread the page. Write the words that help you figure out what **president** means.

_____

_____

3 Comprehension
Cause and Effect

Why does Jane think Abe will make a great president?

_____

_____

Underline the text evidence.

179

1 **Expand Vocabulary**

Reread the page. What two words help you understand what **uncertain** means?

_____

_____

2 **Comprehension**
Cause and Effect

Talk about what happens to Jane as she begins to learn to read. What is the cause?

Underline the effect.

3 **Organization** ⒶⒸⓉ

What words help you figure out when events in the story take place?

_____

_____

At first, Jane was **nervous** about learning to read. She felt shy and **uncertain**. But, this was only **temporary** and didn't last long. She was learning to read. As a result, her nervousness began to **disappear**. One afternoon, Abe surprised Jane. To her **amazement**, he gave her his favorite book about George Washington.

Peter Ferguson

"Thank you," said Jane. "I never want to stop reading."

Years later, Jane read that Abe had been elected president. Jane thought about the day she tripped over his legs. She smiled because that was the day that changed her life.

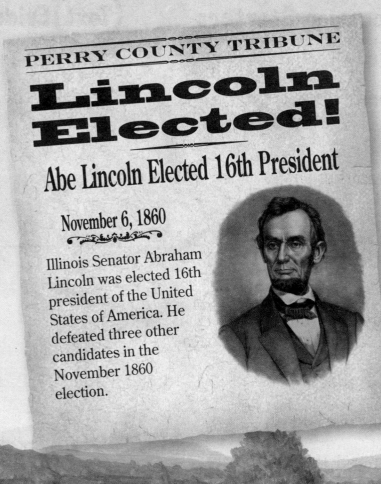

PERRY COUNTY TRIBUNE

Lincoln Elected!

Abe Lincoln Elected 16th President

November 6, 1860

Illinois Senator Abraham Lincoln was elected 16th president of the United States of America. He defeated three other candidates in the November 1860 election.

Text Evidence

1 Organization ACT

Draw a box around the words that show time order. What other detail helps you know when the story takes place?

_____

_____

2 Comprehension
Cause and Effect

Reread the second paragraph. _She smiled_ is the effect. **Underline** the cause. Write the signal word.

_____

3 Organization ACT

Look at the illustrations on pages 180 and 181. How does the author use illustrations to show that time has passed?

181

Respond to Reading

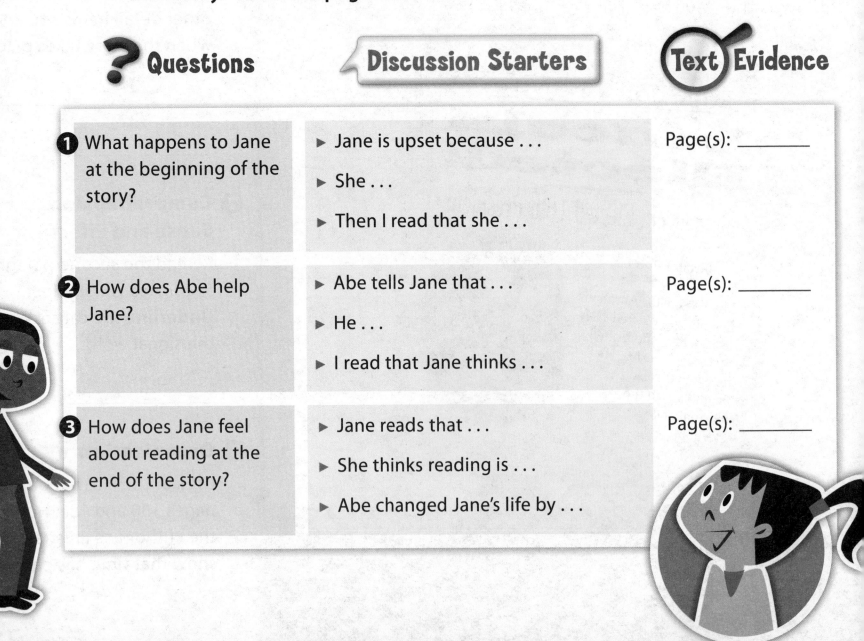

COLLABORATE

Discuss Work with a partner. Use the discussion starters to answer the questions about "Jane's Discovery." Write the page numbers.

? Questions

Discussion Starters

Text Evidence

1 What happens to Jane at the beginning of the story?

▶ Jane is upset because . . .

▶ She . . .

▶ Then I read that she . . .

Page(s): _____

2 How does Abe help Jane?

▶ Abe tells Jane that . . .

▶ He . . .

▶ I read that Jane thinks . . .

Page(s): _____

3 How does Jane feel about reading at the end of the story?

▶ Jane reads that . . .

▶ She thinks reading is . . .

▶ Abe changed Jane's life by . . .

Page(s): _____

Mike Moran

Write Review your notes. Then use text evidence to answer the question below.

How does Abe Lincoln change the way Jane thinks?

At the beginning of the story, Jane _____

_____

_____

Abe Lincoln helps her _____

_____

Jane _____

_____

_____

At the end of the story _____

_____

_____

Write About Reading

Shared Read

Read an Analysis **Cause and Effect** Read Tom's paragraph about "Jane's Discovery." He analyzes how well he thinks the author uses signal words to show causes and effects.

Student Model

Topic Sentence

Circle the topic sentence. What does Tom tell?

Evidence

Draw a box around the text evidence. Is there any other evidence in the story Tom can tell about?

Concluding Statement

Underline the concluding statement. Why is it a good way to end the paragraph?

> In "Jane's Discovery," the author does a good job using signal words to show causes and effects. At the beginning, Jane is upset, so she runs and runs. She is not paying attention. As a result, she trips over Abe. The signal words help me understand that Jane trips because she was not looking. The author's use of signal words helps me find causes and effects in the story.

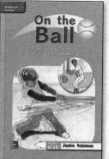

Leveled Reader

Write an Analysis Cause and Effect Write about "On the Ball." How well do you think the author uses signal words to show causes and effects in Chapter 3?

In _____

I think the author uses signal words to show _____

_____

For example, the author says that _____

_____

_____

The author also says that _____

_____

I think the author _____

_____

_____

Topic Sentence

☐ Include the title of the text you read.

Evidence

☐ Tell how the author uses signal words to show cause and effect.

☐ Give examples.

Concluding Statement

☐ Restate how the author shows cause and effect.

? Essential Question

What do we know about Earth and its neighbors?

Go Digital!

Write words that tell about how people make new discoveries.

Discoveries

 Describe how you made a new discovery. Use words you wrote.

(l) Blend Images/Alamy; (r) NASA, ESA, and M. Livio (STScI)

Vocabulary

 Work with a partner to complete each activity.

1 warmth

What might you wear for *warmth*? Write two examples here.

_____

_____

2 solar system

The Sun is in our *solar system*. Tell something else you know about our *solar system*.

_____

_____

3 temperature

Why is it important to know what the *temperature* outside is?

_____

_____

4 amount

Where would you keep a large *amount* of water?

_____

5 surface

Describe the *surface* of an ice skating rink.

_____

_____

6 astronomy

Barry learned about the Moon in *astronomy* class. What is *astronomy* the study of?

_____

7 **support**

Ryan wants to *support* his sister's soccer team. Name some things he can do.

8 **globe**

Draw a picture of something that is shaped like a *globe*.

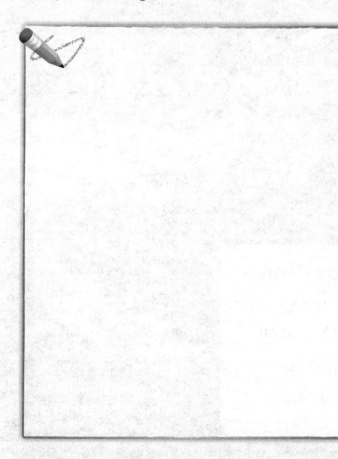

High-Frequency Words

▶ **Read** each word. **Spell** each word. **Write** each word.

found _____

go _____

into _____

look _____

put _____

some _____

Read the story. **Circle** high-frequency words.

Sheila likes to (look) up into the night sky. She found a spot in the grass. She put down a blanket. Sheila knows some of the names of the stars in the sky.

My Notes

Read "Earth and Its Neighbors." Use this page to take notes as you read.

_____

_____

_____

_____

_____

_____

_____

_____

_____

_____

Earth and Its Neighbors

? Essential Question

How do we know about Earth and its neighbors?

Read about how we learned about space.

Galileo studies the sky. He uses his new telescope.

The Sun is hot. Without the Sun, Earth would be cold and dark. How do we know this?

Thanks to an astronomer named Galileo, we know a lot about the Sun and our **solar system**.

Telescopes: Looking Up

Galileo made a very strong **telescope**. He used it to look into space and study the sky. Galileo saw the rocky surface of the Moon. He **discovered** spots on the surface of the Sun.

The Moon is the Earth's closest neighbor.

Text Evidence

1 **Connection of Ideas** (A)(C)(T)

Look at the illustration on page 190. **Circle** details that help you know that Galileo lived a long time ago.

2 **Expand Vocabulary**

Discovered means *found out for the first time*. List one thing Galileo *discovered*.

_____

3 **Comprehension**

Main Idea and Key Details

Reread "Telescopes: Looking Up." List one key detail that tells about Galileo.

_____

Underline the text evidence.

191

Text Evidence

① Comprehension

Main Idea and Key Details

Reread the third paragraph. **Underline** the key details about satellites. What do the details have in common?

② Expand Vocabulary

What word helps you understand what **information** means?

_____

③ Comprehension

Main Idea and Key Details

Use the key details to tell the main idea of "Satellites: A Step Closer."

_____

_____

_____

Astronomy is the study of space. The study of space began with the telescope. But astronomers wanted to look at the sky more closely. They made stronger telescopes. But they still had many questions.

Satellites: A Step Closer

In 1958, the first American **satellite** was put into space. It was an exciting day for America.

Soon, many satellites circled the **globe**. They took photographs of the Earth, the Moon, stars, and other planets. They collected a large **amount** of **information**, or facts, about space.

A satellite takes off.

Astronomers learned many things from satellites. So they sent more into space. But astronomers wanted to know even more. That's why they found a way to put a man on the moon.

One Giant Leap

Alan Shepard was the first American astronaut. He rode a rocket into space and back. His short trip was a big success. It proved humans could go into space.

After Shepard, more astronauts went into space. Some **orbited**, or went around, the Earth. Some walked on the Moon. They took pictures and collected Moon rocks. They asked questions. Did the Sun's **warmth** heat the moon? Could the Moon **support** life someday?

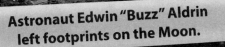

Astronaut Edwin "Buzz" Aldrin left footprints on the Moon.

Aldrin brought home this Moon rock.

(l) MPI/Archive Photos/Getty Images; (r) NASA-JSC

Text Evidence

1 Connection of Ideas Ⓐ Ⓒ Ⓣ

Reread the first paragraph. How did Alan Shepard help scientists learn more about space?

_____

Circle the text evidence.

2 Expand Vocabulary

Reread the second paragraph. What words help you figure out what **orbited** means?

_____

3 Comprehension
Main Idea and Key Details

Reread "One Giant Leap." **Underline** key details that tell how astronauts help us learn about space. Tell what these details have in common.

Text Evidence

1 Connection of Ideas A C T

What problem did astronomers have?

_____

_____

Draw a box around what astronomers did next.

2 Expand Vocabulary

Circle the word that helps you know what **gigantic** means.

3 Comprehension

Main Idea and Key Details

Reread the section, "Hubble and Beyond." **Underline** key details. What is the main idea?

_____

_____

Astronomers learned a lot. But they wanted to get closer. Soon they found a way!

Hubble and Beyond

Astronomers created a **gigantic**, or large, telescope. It is called the Hubble Telescope, and it takes pictures of stars and planets. The Hubble helps astronomers study Earth and its neighbors.

The Hubble orbits Earth. One orbit takes 96 minutes.

Frank Whitney/The Image Bank/Getty Images

More Discoveries Every Day

Scientists still ask questions about space. They will continue to **explore** and find answers.

What Can We See?

With Our Eyes	With a Simple Telescope	With the Hubble Telescope
The Moon	Craters on the Moon	Planets outside our solar system
The Sun	Sunspots	Stars bigger than the Sun
Mars	Clouds around Jupiter	Jupiter's surface

The Hubble took this picture. It shows an exploding star.

Text Evidence

1 Expand Vocabulary

What words help you figure out what **explore** means?

_____

2 Connection of Ideas Ⓐ Ⓒ Ⓣ

Look at the chart. What can we see with our eyes?

_____

_____

_____

3 Connection of Ideas Ⓐ Ⓒ Ⓣ

Read the chart. Name one thing in space we can see with the Hubble Telescope.

_____

Circle one thing we can see with a simple telescope.

Respond to Reading

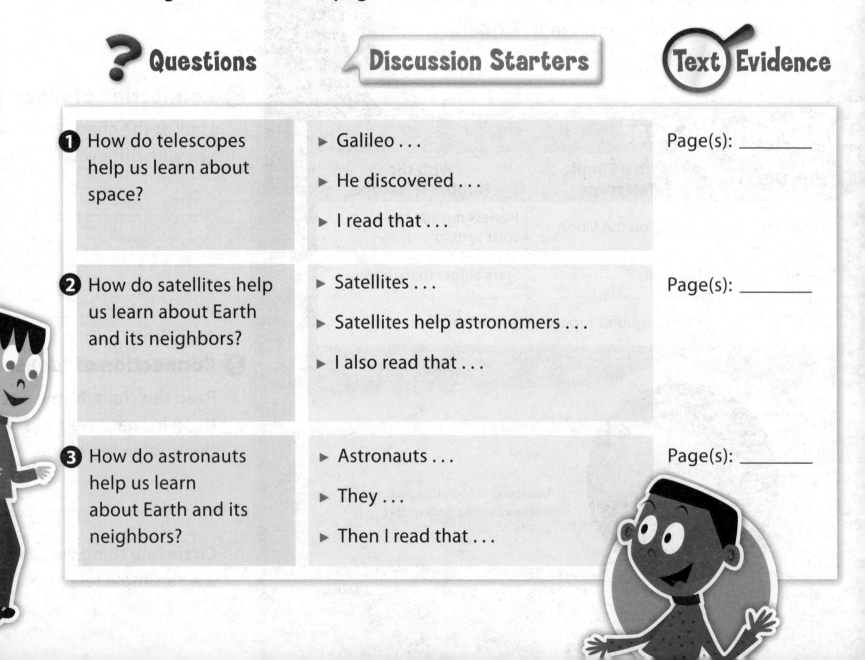

COLLABORATE

Discuss Work with a partner. Use the discussion starters to answer the questions about "Earth and Its Neighbors." Write the page numbers.

? Questions · **Discussion Starters** · **Text Evidence**

1 How do telescopes help us learn about space?

► Galileo . . .

► He discovered . . .

► I read that . . .

Page(s): _____

2 How do satellites help us learn about Earth and its neighbors?

► Satellites . . .

► Satellites help astronomers . . .

► I also read that . . .

Page(s): _____

3 How do astronauts help us learn about Earth and its neighbors?

► Astronauts . . .

► They . . .

► Then I read that . . .

Page(s): _____

Mike Moran

Write Review your notes. Then use text evidence to answer the questions below.

How do we learn about Earth and its neighbors?

Telescopes help us learn about Earth and its neighbors by _____

_____

_____

Satellites _____

_____

Another way we learn about Earth and it neighbors is _____

_____

_____

Scientists will _____

_____

_____

Write About Reading

Shared Read

Read Harry's paragraph about "Earth and Its Neighbors." He analyzes how the author uses key details that go together to tell the main idea.

Student Model

Topic Sentence

Circle the topic sentence. What does Harry tell?

Evidence

Draw a box around the text evidence. Is there any other evidence Harry can tell about?

Concluding Statement

Underline the concluding statement. Why is it a good way to end the paragraph?

In "Earth and Its Neighbors," the author uses key details that go together to tell the main idea. I read that astronomers send satellites into space. The satellites take pictures and collect information. Scientists learn about space. The author uses key details that go together and tell that satellites help us learn about space.

Leveled Reader

In _____

the author uses key details about _____

_____

For example, the author says that _____

_____

The author also says that _____

_____

These key details work together to _____

_____

_____

Essential Question

What ideas can we get from nature?

Go Digital!

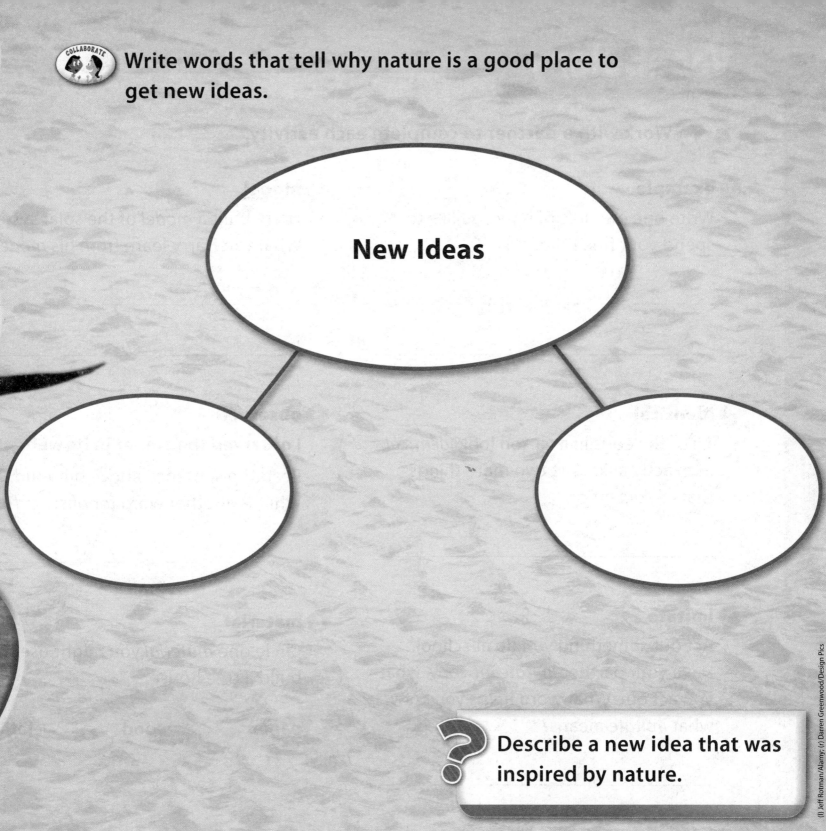

COLLABORATE Write words that tell why nature is a good place to get new ideas.

New Ideas

? Describe a new idea that was inspired by nature.

Vocabulary

 Work with a partner to complete each activity.

1 example

Write one *example* of how you like to spend your free time.

_____

_____

2 identical

All of the eggs in a carton look *identical*, or exactly alike. List two more things that look *identical*.

_____

3 imitate

Act out something you do at school. Have your partner *imitate*, or copy, what you act out. What word helps you know what *imitate* means?

_____

4 model

Harry built a *model* of the solar system. What can Harry learn from his *model*?

_____

_____

5 observed

I *observed* the spider in its web.

Read the sentence above out loud. What is another word for *observed*?

_____

6 material

Circle one *material* you might use to build a tree house.

paper   **wood**   **cloth**

7 effective

Another word for *effective* is useful.
Circle two more synonyms for *effective*.

hard   good   helpful

8 similar

Draw two things that look *similar*.

High-Frequency Words

▶ **Read** each word. **Spell** each word.
Write each word.

away _____

eat _____

good _____

other _____

out _____

use _____

Read the story. **Circle** high-frequency
words.

Barry saw a big fish try to (eat) a
small fish. The small fish swam away.
It hid under a rock and did
not come out. Barry thought
that was a good idea.

My Notes

Read "Bats Did It First." Use this page to take notes as you read.

BATS DID IT FIRST

Essential Question

What ideas can we get from nature?

Read about how bats inspired a new invention.

Nature is full of great ideas. Many inventors and scientists go outside to get **inspiration**. They can **imitate**, or copy, what they see in nature.

One great invention was inspired by bats. It's a special cane. It helps blind people get around.

This boy is blind. He uses a special cane to help him get around.

❶ Expand Vocabulary

Reread the first paragraph. **Circle** the words that help you figure out what **inspiration** is.

❷ Comprehension
Main Idea and Key Details

Underline two details in the first paragraph that tell about how many inventors and scientists get new ideas.

❸ Comprehension
Main Idea and Key Details

Reread the key details. What do they have in common?

_____

_____

What is the main idea?

_____

Text Evidence

1 Expand Vocabulary

What word helps you figure out what **locate** means?

_____

2 Comprehension

Main Idea and Key Details

Reread "Canes Lead the Way." **Underline** key details that tell how blind people use canes. What do the key details have in common?

_____

_____

_____

3 Sentence Structure (A)(C)(T)

Reread the third paragraph. **Circle** one sentence the author uses to get you to keep reading.

Canes Lead the Way

Many blind people use canes. They tap their canes on the ground in front of them. This helps them **locate**, or find, things. Canes help them move around safely.

The new cane is different. It sends out sound waves, or signals. These signals are almost **identical** to the ones bats use when they fly.

How Bats Get Around

The scientist that came up with the new cane **observed** the way bats fly. The bats make sounds that people can't hear. These sounds help bats get around. Here's how it works.

milehightraveler/iStock/Getty Images

Bats send sound waves out their mouth or nose. These sound waves hit objects. Then they bounce back as an echo. The echo tells the bats how far away an object is. This helps bats find bugs to eat. It also keeps bats from bumping into trees and other bats.

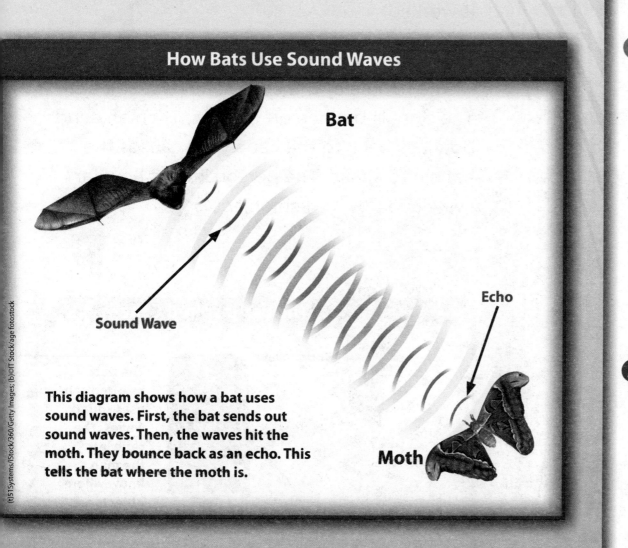

How Bats Use Sound Waves

Bat

Sound Wave

Echo

Moth

This diagram shows how a bat uses sound waves. First, the bat sends out sound waves. Then, the waves hit the moth. They bounce back as an echo. This tells the bat where the moth is.

(t)515ystems/iStock/360/Getty Images; (b)IT Stock/age fotostock

Text Evidence

❶ **Comprehension**
Main Idea and Key Details

Underline key details that tell how bats use sound waves to get around.

❷ **Comprehension**
Main Idea and Key Details

Reread the key details. Think about what they have in common. Write the main idea.

_____

_____

_____

❸ **Sentence Structure** Ⓐ Ⓒ Ⓣ

Reread the caption. What happens after bats send out sound waves?

_____

207

Text Evidence

1 **Expand Vocabulary**

Reread the first paragraph.
Draw a box around a synonym
for **ordinary**.

2 **Sentence Structure** **ACT**

Reread "A Batty Idea." **Circle**
the sentence that shows what
the author thinks of the new
cane.

What does the author think
about the new cane?

_____

_____

3 **Comprehension**
Main Idea and Key Details

Reread the second paragraph.
Underline key details that tell
about how the cane works.
Write the main idea.

_____

A Batty Idea

The scientist who invented the new cane
observed bats. The new cane used a **similar**
idea. He started with an **ordinary** white cane.
He made a **model** of the simple cane. Then
he built a cane that was light and strong. He
added sound waves. Last, he tested the cane.
It worked!

How the Cane Works

The handle of the cane sends out signals.
The signals bounce off objects. Then an echo
bounces back to the cane. This causes the
handle to shake. The person knows how far
away and how big an object is.

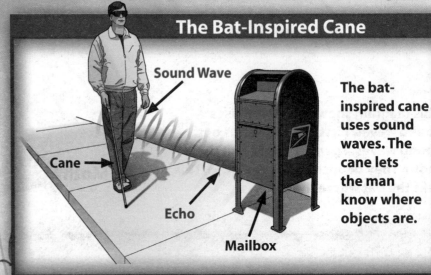

The Bat-Inspired Cane

Sound Wave

Cane

Echo

Mailbox

The bat-
inspired cane
uses sound
waves. The
cane lets
the man
know where
objects are.

Steve Schell

Some **amazing** and wonderful ideas come from nature! This cane is a good **example**.

This scientist is studying bats.

Text Evidence

1 Expand Vocabulary

Draw a box around a word that means almost the same as **amazing.**

2 Sentence Structure Ⓐ Ⓒ Ⓣ

What words does the author use to show what he thinks about the new cane?

_____

_____

3 Comprehension

Main Idea and Key Details

Reread key details in the selection. Use what they have in common to tell the main idea of "Bats Did It First."

_____

_____

209

Respond to Reading

COLLABORATE **Discuss** Work with a partner. Use the discussion starts to answer the questions about "Bats Did It First." Write the page numbers.

? Questions · **Discussion Starters** · **Text Evidence**

❶ How do scientists get ideas from nature?

▶ Many inventors . . .

▶ They . . .

▶ I read that . . .

Page(s): _____

❷ How did bats inspire a cane to help blind people?

▶ Scientists . . .

▶ When bats fly, they . . .

▶ I read that . . .

Page(s): _____

❸ How does the new invention work?

▶ The handle of the cane . . .

▶ The person . . .

▶ I know this because . . .

Page(s): _____

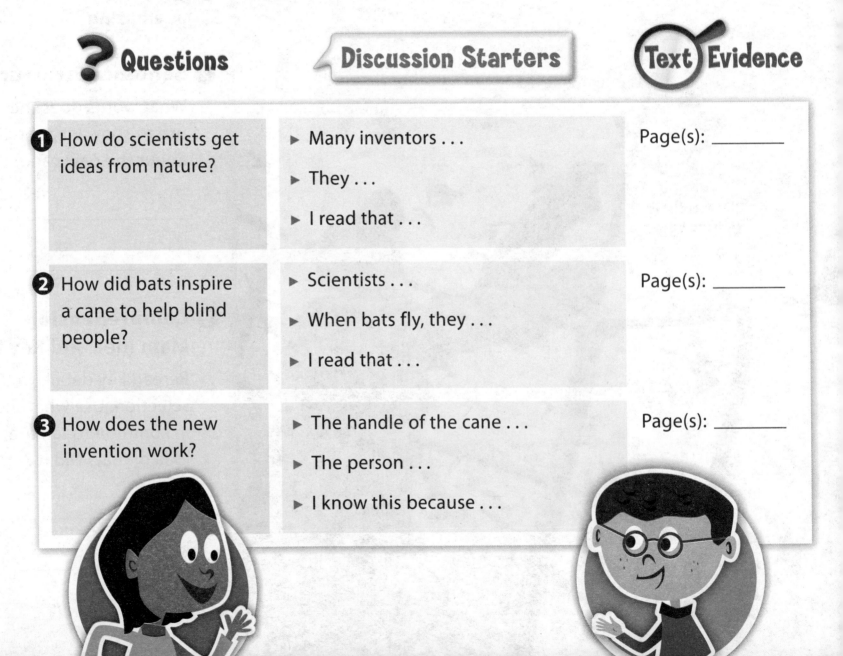

✎ Write Review your notes. Then use text evidence to answer the question below.

What is one idea that comes from nature?

One idea that comes from nature is _____

_____

_____

A scientist _____

_____

The cane _____

_____

_____

It helps people because _____

_____

_____

Write About Reading

Shared Read

Read Ellen's paragraph about "Bats Did it First." She analyzes whether the author uses enough key details to tell the main idea.

Student Model

Topic Sentence

Circle the topic sentence. What does Ellen tell?

Evidence

Draw a box around the text evidence. Is there any other evidence in the selection Ellen can tell about?

Concluding Statement

Underline the concluding statement. Why is it a good way to end the paragraph?

In "Bats Did it First," the author uses many key details that go together to help me figure out the main idea. In the section "How the Cane Works," I read that that the cane's handle sends out signals. They bounce off objects and make the handle shake. This warns people. The author gives enough key details to help me figure out that the main idea tells how the new cane works.

Leveled Reader

Write about "Inspired by Nature." Do you think the author uses enough key details to support the main idea of Chapter 1?

In _____

I think the author uses enough key details to

show _____

_____

For example, the author says that _____

_____

The author also says that _____

_____

I think these details support _____

_____

Topic Sentence

☐ Include the title of the text you read.

Evidence

☐ Tell how the author uses key details.
☐ Give examples.

Concluding Statement

☐ Restate how the author uses enough key details to tell the main idea.

213

Essential Question

How is each event in history unique?

Go Digital!

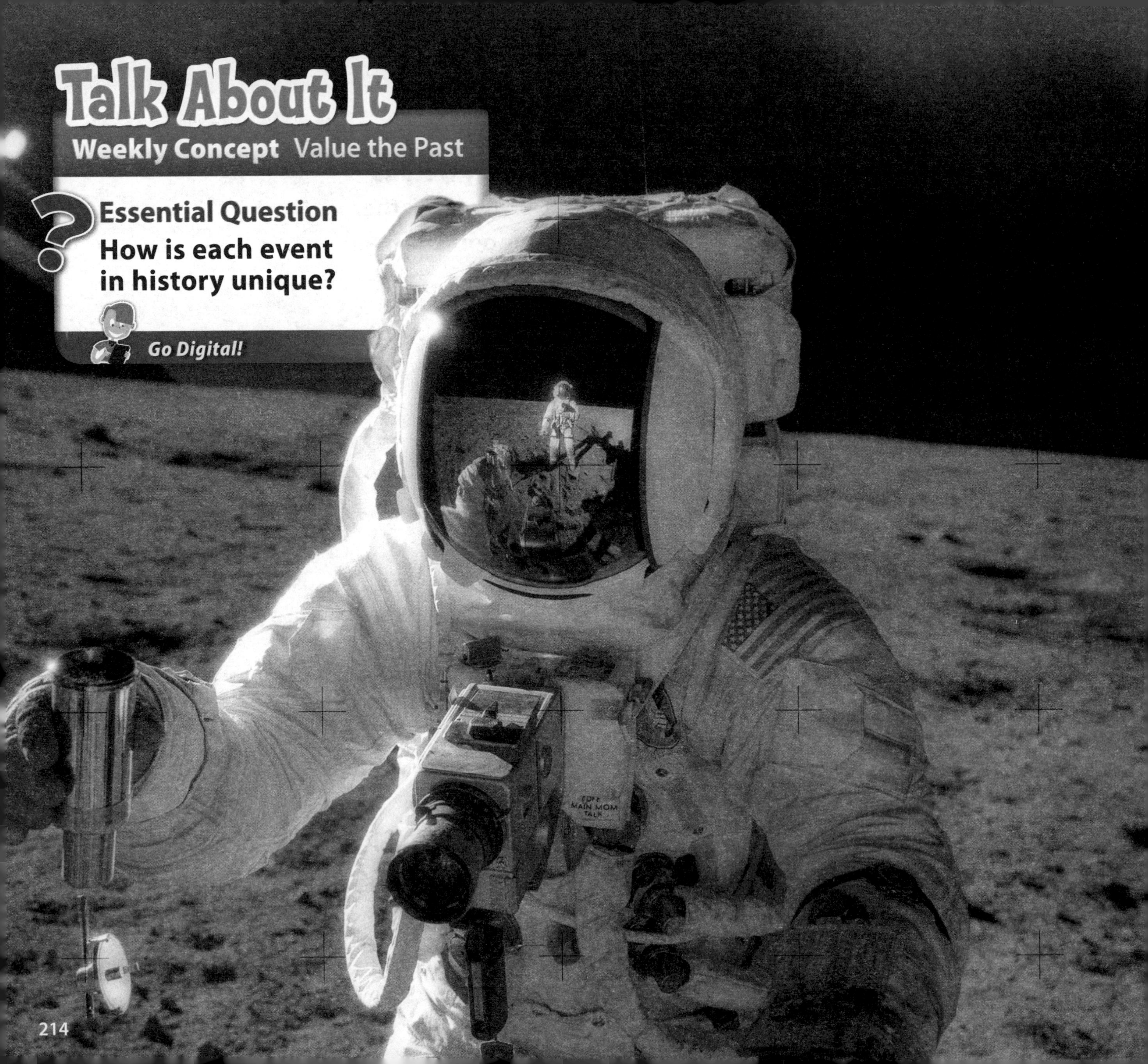

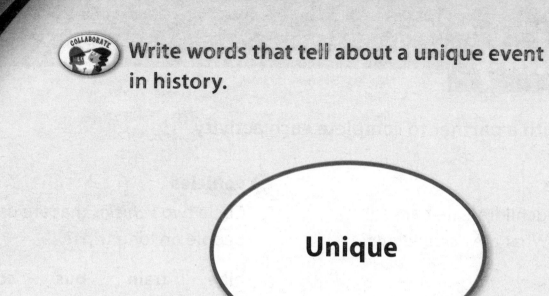

COLLABORATE Write words that tell about a unique event in history.

Unique

 Describe the event and what makes it unique. Use words from above.

Vocabulary

1 descendants

Denise's grandchildren are her *descendants*. What are *descendants*?

_____

_____

2 appreciate

Ben and Kim *appreciate* their teacher and want to show him how much they are thankful for everything he does. Circle the words that help you understand what *appreciate* means.

3 boomed

The sale of umbrellas *boomed* when it rained. Name two more things that might sell when it rains.

_____

4 vehicles

Circle two *vehicles* that are used to take people on long trips?

bike   train   bus   scooter

5 pioneers

The *pioneers*, or settlers, traveled a long way to their new home.

Read the sentence above out loud. What is another word for *pioneers*?

_____

6 emigration

Many people who leave their own country to live in a new one know that *emigration* is difficult. What words help you understand what *emigration* is?

_____

_____

216

7 agreeable

Circle the suffix in *agreeable*? What does *agreeable* mean?

_____

_____

8 transportation

Draw a picture of your favorite form of *transportation*.

High-Frequency Words

▶ **Read** each word. **Spell** each word. **Write** each word.

away _____

got _____

first _____

that _____

their _____

our _____

Read the story. **Circle** high-frequency words.

Jeb's family moved (away.) First they packed their things. Then they got on a train. That was a brave thing to do.

My Notes

Read "The Long Road to Oregon." Use this page to take notes as you read.

_____

_____

_____

_____

_____

_____

_____

_____

_____

_____

Pioneers rode in covered wagons like these.

? Essential Question

How is each event in history unique?

Read to see how the pioneers got to Oregon.

The Long Road to Oregon

In 1843, more than 800 people went on a trip, or **journey**. They traveled west from Missouri to Oregon. These **pioneers** had 120 wagons. This was one of the first wagon trains to travel the Oregon Trail.

Land of Promise

Life was hard in Missouri. Bad weather caused crops to die. Businesses closed. As a result, many people could not find jobs.

Americans wanted a better life. They wanted to live in a place where the soil was rich. They wanted to live where the weather was more **agreeable** and pleasant.

The United States government was giving free land to pioneers. Then many people traveled to Oregon.

This map shows the Oregon Trail in 1843.

The Oregon Trail

Oregon City
OREGON COUNTRY
UNORGANIZED TERRITORY
IOWA
MEXICAN TERRITORY
Independence
MISSOURI
REPUBLIC OF TEXAS

KEY
— Trail
• Cities

1 **Expand Vocabulary**

Reread the first paragraph. **Draw a box** around words that help you understand what **journey** means.

2 **Comprehension**
Sequence

Reread the fourth paragraph. What happened after the government gave free land to pioneers? **Underline** it.

3 **Connection of Ideas** **A C T**

Look at the map. Where do the pioneers start their journey?

_____

_____

Circle where the trail begins.

Text Evidence

1 Expand Vocabulary

Draw a box around the word that helps you understand what **prepared** means.

2 Comprehension
Sequence

Reread "Getting Ready to Go." What do the families do first?

_____

Circle the signal word that tells time order.

3 Comprehension
Sequence

Reread "A Long, Hard Journey." What did families do after they hooked up the oxen?

_____

Circle the signal word that tells time order.

Getting Ready to Go

Emigration would be difficult. Oregon was more than 2,000 miles away. The trails were dusty and bumpy. The trip would take at least five months. The pioneers needed to be **prepared** so they would be ready to go.

First they gathered their cows and chickens. Then they packed food, pots, tools, and seeds.

Covered wagons were used for **transportation**. The wagons were stuffed with what they would need. There was little room for anything else. As a result, children left books, toys, and most of their clothes behind.

A Long, Hard Journey

It took weeks to get ready. First, families hooked oxen to their wagons. Oxen were strong and could pull the heavy **vehicles**. Next, families joined together.

All the wagons formed a wagon train. Most people walked. Sick or tired pioneers rode in the wagons.

Dirty water, sickness, and dust storms made the journey hard. But the pioneers were determined. As a result, they finally reached their new home in Oregon.

A reenactment on the trail

(b) Greg Ryan/Alamy; (c) Oleksiy Maksymenko/Alamy; (inset) Nik Wheeler/Alamy

A New Life in Oregon

When the pioneers got to Oregon, they cleared land and built houses. Then they planted crops. Towns grew. People opened stores and restaurants. Businesses **boomed**. They had found a better life!

Many people in Oregon today are **descendants** of the brave pioneers. They **appreciate** their family's hard work and courage. They are grateful for the Oregon Trail.

Learn Your History!

History is the study of people and events from the past. It helps us understand some of the **difficult** and challenging things people did. You can read stories written by the pioneers. You can read about explorers. Learning about history can be more exciting than a movie!

Part of the Oregon Trail today

Text Evidence

❶ Comprehension
Sequence

Reread the first paragraph. What did the pioneers do after they cleared land and built houses?

_____

Underline the text evidence.

❷ Expand Vocabulary

Reread the sidebar. **Draw a box** around the word that helps you understand what **difficult** means.

❸ Connection of Ideas A C T

Reread the sidebar. What does the author think about history?

_____

Circle the text evidence.

Respond to Reading

Discuss Work with a partner. Use the discussion starters to answer the questions about "The Long Road to Oregon." Write the page numbers.

? Questions | **Discussion Starters** | **Text Evidence**

1 Why do the pioneers go to Oregon?	▶ Life was . . . ▶ The pioneers . . . ▶ I also read that . . .	Page(s): _____
2 How do the pioneers get ready to go to Oregon?	▶ First they . . . ▶ Then . . . ▶ I read that the trip was . . .	Page(s): _____
3 What do the pioneers do when they reach Oregon?	▶ First the pioneers . . . ▶ Then they . . . ▶ Many people in Oregon today . . .	Page(s): _____

Write Review your notes. Then use text evidence to answer the question below.

How was the journey on the Oregon Trail unique?

Pioneers left Missouri because _____

_____

First they _____

_____

The journey was _____

_____

_____

When they got to Oregon, they _____

_____

_____

Write About Reading

Shared Read

Read an Analysis **Sequence** Read Sari's paragraph about "The Long Road to Oregon." She analyzes how the author uses signal words to show the sequence of events.

Student Model

In "The Long Road to Oregon," the author uses signal words to show the events in time order. First I read that life in Missouri was hard. Then, the pioneers packed and got ready. Next, they travelled a long time. Finally, they reached Oregon. The author tells the story of these pioneers using signal words.

Topic Sentence

Circle the topic sentence. What does Sari tell?

Evidence

Draw a box around the text evidence. Is there any other evidence Sari could tell about?

Concluding Statement

Underline the concluding statement. Why is it a good way to end the paragraph?

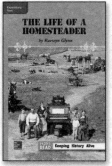

Leveled Reader

Write an Analysis **Sequence** Write about "The Life of a Homesteader." How does the author use signal words to show the sequence of events in Chapter 1?

In _____

the author _____

_____

For example, the author says that _____

_____

_____

The author also says that _____

_____

These signal words support _____

_____

Topic Sentence

☐ Include the title of the text you read.

Evidence

☐ Tell how the author uses signal words to show the sequence of events in the story.

☐ Give examples.

Concluding Statement

☐ Restate how the author shows the sequence of events using signal words.

Unit 4

Meet the Challenge

The Big Idea

What are different ways to meet challenges?

Talk About It

Weekly Concept Choices

Essential Question
What choices are good for us?

Go Digital!

Write words that tell why it is important to make smart choices.

Smart Choices

$\downarrow$

$\downarrow$

$\downarrow$

 Describe a smart choice you made today. Use words you wrote above.

Vocabulary

 Work with a partner to complete each activity.

1 **flavorful**

Underline the base word in *flavorful*.
Circle the suffix.
What does *flavorful* mean?

_____

2 **luscious**

Wendy ate a sweet and *luscious* pineapple for snack. List two foods that you think are *luscious*.

_____

_____

3 **aroma**

James loves the *aroma* of his grandmother's cooking.

Read the sentence above out loud.
What is another word for *aroma*?

_____

4 **graceful**

The *graceful* deer stepped carefully across the leaves. Name another animal that moves in a *graceful* way.

_____

5 **expect**

Tomorrow is the first day of vacation. I *expect,* or believe, I will go swimming. What word helps you understand what *expect* means?

_____

_____

6 **healthful**

Read the list of foods below. Then circle two examples of *healthful* snacks.

candy   apple

banana   potato chips

7 **interrupted**

The fire alarm *interrupted* our class play. Tell about a time you were *interrupted* by something.

8 **variety**

Draw the *variety* of foods you eat in a day.

High-Utility Words

▶ **Contractions with *not***

A contraction combines a verb with the word *not*. The word *can't* is a contraction for *can not*.

Read the passage. **Circle** the contractions with *not*.

Ray and Juan (don't) know what to eat. Juan can't decide. Ray is hungry, because he hasn't eaten all day. "We can eat cookies," said Ray. "That isn't healthy for you. We should eat carrots instead!" said Juan.

My Notes

Read "Nail Soup." Use this page to take notes as you read.

_____

_____

_____

_____

_____

_____

_____

_____

_____

_____

_____

_____

_____

Nail Soup

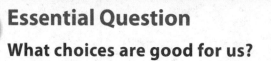

? Essential Question

What choices are good for us?

Read about how choices helped a man and his wife learn a lesson.

Once long ago, Papa and I were walking for miles on a long country road. Finally we saw a farmhouse **surrounded** on all sides by vegetable fields.

"Papa, I'm so hungry," I said.

Papa winked at me. I smiled and nodded. I admired my Papa. I knew he would find us a warm meal. We knocked on the door and a well-dressed man and his wife answered.

"Hello," said Papa. "My son, Erik, is hungry. Could you please spare some food?"

"We have lots of food, but we can't give any away," said the man.

"I can cook my **flavorful** nail soup if you would donate some hot water," said Papa.

"Soup from a nail?" asked the woman. "That's impossible." But the man was curious, so he brought a cup of boiling water.

Illustrator: B Gerardo Suzan

Text Evidence

1 Comprehension

Point of View

Reread the first three paragraphs. **Circle** two details that tell what Erik thinks of Papa.

2 Expand Vocabulary

Reread the fourth paragraph. Someone who is **impolite** is rude or has bad manners. What does Erik think is *impolite*?

_____

_____

_____

3 Genre A C T

What does Papa do to help solve Erik's problem?

_____

_____

Papa dropped a nail into the cup with one **graceful** motion and stirred.

"This smells wonderful," said Papa.

I smiled. Papa was clever and charming. He could do anything!

"Papa, it's **impolite** for me to eat without offering some to everyone," I said. "But there is so little."

"We can spare more water," the man told his wife.

The woman filled a big pot with water and put it on the stove. Papa put the nail in and stirred. He sniffed the air. "The **aroma** is good, but some onions would help."

The woman brought onions, and Papa dropped them into the pot.

"Papa, remember how **luscious** nail soup was with carrots?" I asked.

The man found some carrots. "Add some beets and cabbages, too!" he said.

"And some potatoes and green beans!" the woman **interrupted**. "They are **healthful**, nutritious **contributions**."

The man grabbed a **variety** of spices and meats. "Here, add these!" he said.

When the soup was ready, we sat down to eat.

"This soup is so good," said the woman. "And all from just one nail and water."

Papa had the perfect answer. "What did you **expect**?" he said. "I said it was flavorful."

The man and woman smiled. "We just didn't know that sharing would taste so good!"

Text Evidence

1 Expand Vocabulary

Contributions are things that you add or give to something. Reread pages 234 and 235. **Underline** the man and woman's *contributions* to the soup.

2 Comprehension
Point of View

What does Erik think of Papa?

_____

Circle the text evidence.

3 Genre

Reread the last paragraph. What lesson do the man and his wife learn?

_____

_____

Draw a box around the text evidence.

235

Respond to Reading

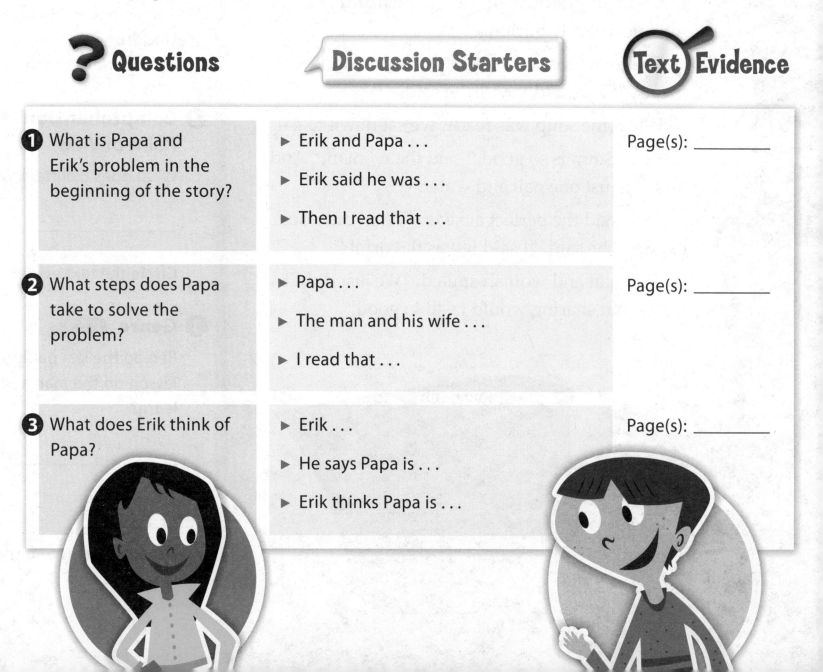

Discuss Work with a partner. Use the discussion starters to answer the questions about "Nail Soup." Write the page numbers.

? Questions

Discussion Starters

Text Evidence

1 What is Papa and Erik's problem in the beginning of the story?

▶ Erik and Papa . . .

▶ Erik said he was . . .

▶ Then I read that . . .

Page(s): _____

2 What steps does Papa take to solve the problem?

▶ Papa . . .

▶ The man and his wife . . .

▶ I read that . . .

Page(s): _____

3 What does Erik think of Papa?

▶ Erik . . .

▶ He says Papa is . . .

▶ Erik thinks Papa is . . .

Page(s): _____

Write Review your notes. Then use text evidence to answer the question below.

Why was making nail soup a smart choice?

Erik and Papa were _____

_____

_____

Papa solves the problem by _____

_____

He _____

_____

_____

Erik thinks Papa is _____

_____

_____

Write About Reading

Shared Read

Point of View Read Melanie's paragraph about "Nail Soup." She analyzes how the author uses details to tell the narrator's point of view.

Student Model

Topic Sentence

Circle the topic sentence. What does Melanie tell?

Evidence

Draw a box around the text evidence. Is there any other evidence in the selection Melanie can tell about?

Concluding Statement

Underline the concluding statement. Why is it a good way to end the paragraph?

In "Nail Soup," the author uses what Papa says and does to tell Erik's point of view. Papa makes a soup with hot water and a nail. Erik says he is clever and charming. The man and his wife add lots of food to the pot. Finally, the soup is finished and they eat. The author uses what Papa says and does to show Erik's point of view that he trusts his father and thinks he can do anything.

Leveled Reader

In _____

the author uses details about the characters and

events to _____

_____

For example, the author shows _____

_____

The author also shows _____

_____

The author shows the narrator's point of view that

_____

_____

Topic Sentence
☐ Include the title of the text you read.

Evidence
☐ Tell how the author uses details to tell the narrator's point of view.
☐ Give examples.

Concluding Statement
☐ Restate how the author uses details to tell the narrator's point of view.

Talk About It

Essential Question

How can you use what you know to help others?

Go Digital!

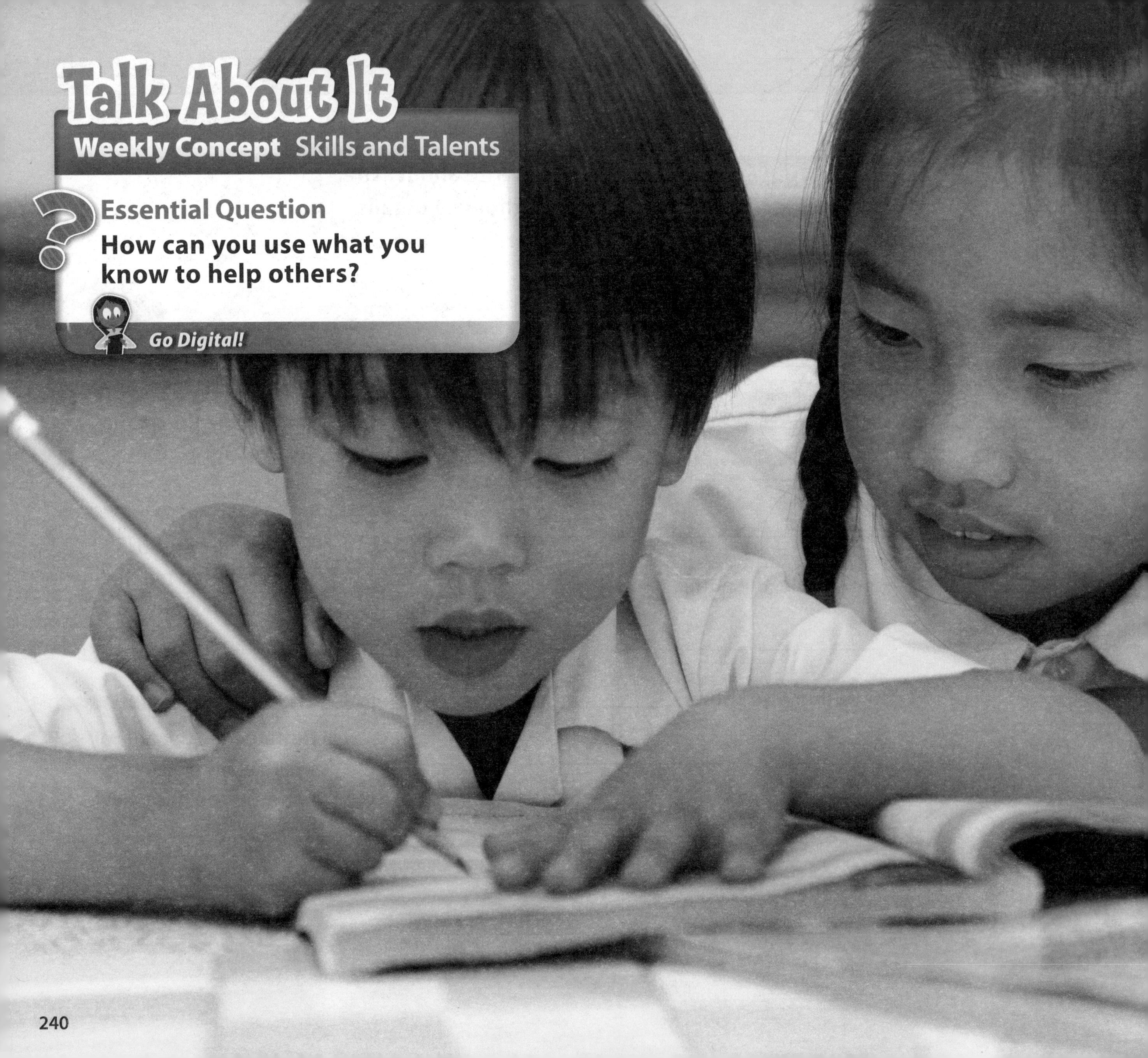

240

Write words that tell about your skills and talents.

Talents

Describe how you can use what you are good at to help someone else.

Derek E. Rothchild/PhotoDisc/Getty Images

Vocabulary

 Work with a partner to complete each activity.

1 attention

What can you do to show someone you are paying *attention*.

_____

_____

2 apologized

Jason *apologized* and told his sister he was sorry for using her skateboard without asking.

Read the sentence above out loud. What words help you understand *apologized*?

_____

3 confidence

Circle two words that describe how you feel if you have a lot of *confidence*.

unsure   calm   sure   shy

4 audience

List two places where you might see an *audience*.

_____

_____

5 achievement

Write a sentence about an *achievement* you are proud of.

_____

_____

6 realized

Mary *realized*, or discovered, she was very good at solving math problems. What word helps you figure out what *realized* means?

_____

7 **embarrassed**

Act out how you might look if you are *embarrassed*.

8 **talents**

Draw a picture of one of your *talents*.

High-Utility Words

▶ **Prepositions**

A preposition comes before a noun or a pronoun. It shows how the noun or pronoun is linked to another word in the sentence. Some common prepositions are *in, on, at, as,* and *over.*

Read the passage. **Circle** the prepositions.

Carl had a lemonade stand (on) the sidewalk. Nobody came.

"Put a sign over your stand," said June. "Put signs at stores."

Soon people stood in line. Carl was happy to have June as a friend.

LEMONADE
10¢

My Notes

Read "The Impossible Pet Show." Use this page to take notes as you read.

_____

_____

_____

_____

_____

_____

_____

_____

_____

_____

_____

_____

The Impossible Pet Show

?

Essential Question

How can you use what you know to help others?

Read how Daniel uses what he knows to save a pet show.

My friend Carla called me on Thursday. "Daniel," she said, "meet me in the park. I have a great idea!" This worried me. Carla's great ideas almost always mean trouble!

My heart sank when I saw Carla because her gigantic dog Perro was with her. I liked everything about Carla *except* Perro. I feel **uncomfortable** and nervous around animals, and I'm **embarrassed** to say that I'm afraid of Carla's dog.

"Let's have a pet show," Carla said. "All our friends can show off their pets' **talents** and the things they do well. You don't have a pet to enter into the show, so you will be the announcer."

Marcin Piwowarski

245

1 Comprehension
Point of View

Reread the first paragraph. **Underline** the details that tells about what Daniel thinks about Carla's idea.

2 Expand Vocabulary

Anxious means nervous or worried. What makes Daniel feel *anxious*?

_____

_____

3 Connection of Ideas Ⓐ Ⓒ Ⓣ

Reread the last paragraph. What causes Daniel to feel calmer?

_____

_____

Circle the text evidence.

"I'm sorry," I **apologized**, "but I can't! Crowds make me nervous, and I don't like animals, remember?"

"That's nonsense," said Carla. "You'll be great!"

Just then, Perro leaped up and almost knocked me down. He slobbered all over me. "Yuck! Down, Perro! Stay!" I shouted. Perro sat as still as a rock. "Wow, you're good at that," said Carla.

Saturday came, and the **audience** arrived. The size of the crowd made me feel even more **anxious**.

I gulped and announced the first pet. So far, everything was perfect. I was feeling calmer. I **realized** being an announcer wasn't so bad after all.

Then it was Carla and Perro's turn.

"Sit, Perro," she said. He didn't sit.

Perro was not paying **attention** to Carla. He was watching Jack's bunnies. Suddenly, Perro leaped at them. They knocked over Pudgy, the hamster's, cage. Pudgy escaped and ran around in circles while Kyle's dog howled. This was a disaster, and I had to do something.

"Sit!" I shouted. "Quiet!" I **ordered**. "Stay!" I commanded. The animals stopped and the audience froze.

"Daniel, that was incredible," said Carla. "You got the pets to settle down. That's quite an **achievement**."

That was the end of our show. But now I have more **confidence** when I speak in front of people. Perro and I have become great friends. I also discovered my talent.

Text Evidence

❶ Connection of Ideas Ⓐ Ⓒ Ⓣ

Reread the third paragraph. **Circle** what Perro does that causes the other animals to escape, run around, and howl?

❷ Expand Vocabulary

Reread the fourth paragraph. **Draw a box** around a word that means almost the same as **ordered**.

❸ Comprehension
Point of View

What does Daniel think about speaking in front of people at the end of the story?

_____

_____

Underline the details.

Respond to Reading

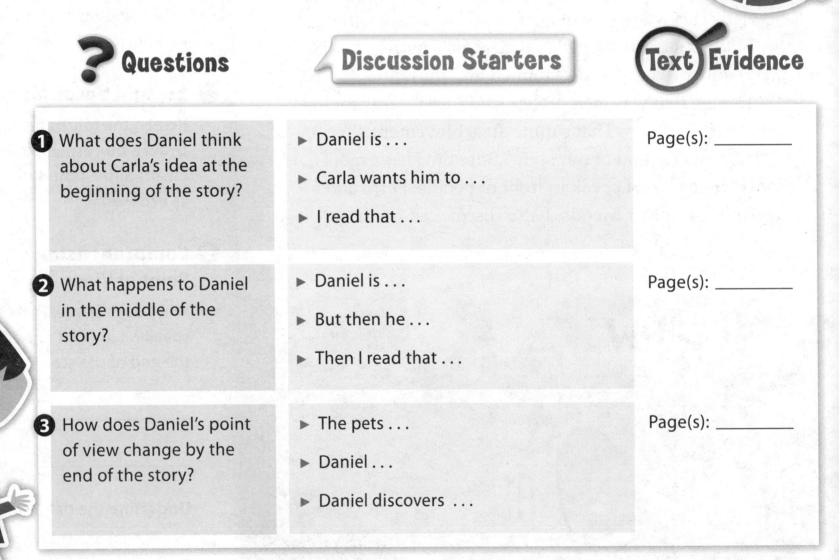

Discuss Work with a partner. Use the discussion starters to answer the questions about "The Impossible Pet Show." Write the page numbers.

? Questions	Discussion Starters	Text Evidence
1 What does Daniel think about Carla's idea at the beginning of the story?	▶ Daniel is . . . ▶ Carla wants him to . . . ▶ I read that . . .	Page(s): _____
2 What happens to Daniel in the middle of the story?	▶ Daniel is . . . ▶ But then he . . . ▶ Then I read that . . .	Page(s): _____
3 How does Daniel's point of view change by the end of the story?	▶ The pets . . . ▶ Daniel . . . ▶ Daniel discovers . . .	Page(s): _____

Mike Moran

248

Write Review your notes. Then use text evidence to answer the question below.

How does Daniel use what he knows to help others?

In the beginning, Daniel thinks _____

_____

_____

Then, he learns he can _____

_____

This skill helps him _____

_____

_____

At the end Daniel helps others by _____

_____

_____

Marcin Piwowarski

249

Write About Reading

Shared Read

Read an Analysis **Point of View** Read Cassie's paragraph about "The Impossible Pet Show." She gives her opinion about whether the author gives enough details to figure out Daniel's point of view.

Student Model

Topic Sentence

Circle the topic sentence. What does Cassie tell?

Evidence

Draw a box around the text evidence. Is there any other evidence in the selection Cassie can tell about?

Concluding Statement

Underline the concluding statement. Why is it a good way to end the paragraph?

In "The Impossible Pet Show," the author gives enough details about Daniel for me figure out what he thinks about being an announcer. Daniel is nervous around animals and crowds. He does not want to be the announcer. But Daniel learns he is good at it. He calms the pets down. The author gives enough details about Daniel and it helps me figure out that he thinks being an announcer is not that bad.

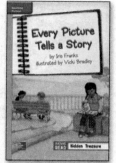

Leveled Reader

Write an Analysis **Author's Point of View** Write about "Every Picture Tells a Story." Do you think the author gives enough details for you to figure out the narrator's point of view in Chapter 2?

In _____

I think the author _____

_____

For example, the author says that _____

_____

The author also says that _____

_____

_____

I think the author _____

_____

Topic Sentence

☐ Include the title of the text you read.

Evidence

☐ Tell whether the author gives enough details to help you figure out the narrator's point of view.

☐ Give examples.

Concluding Statement

☐ Restate whether the author gives enough details for you to figure out point of view.

Essential Question

How do animals adapt to challenges in their habitat?

Go Digital!

COLLABORATE Write words that tell about different ways animals adapt.

[ ]

[ ]

Adaptations

? Describe an animal and its adaptation. Use words you wrote above.

Vocabulary

 Work with a partner to complete each activity.

1 related

Lions are *related* to cats because they are part of the same family. Name someone you are *related* to.

_____

2 prefer

Do you *prefer* swimming or hiking? Name two more activities you *prefer*.

_____

_____

3 excellent

Jill won the spelling bee because she is an *excellent* speller.

Read the sentence above aloud. Write a word that means almost the same as *excellent*.

_____

4 competition

Jerry's team went to the *competition,* or contest, ready to win. What word helps you understand what *competition* means?

_____

5 environment

Write two things plants must have in their *environment* to live.

_____

_____

6 alert

My sister has an alarm clock to *alert* her when it's time to wake up. Name two things that *alert* us of danger.

_____

_____

7 **protection**

Name some things you use for *protection* when you ride a bike or skateboard.

_____

8 **shelter**

Design a *shelter* for camping outdoors. Draw it here.

High-Utility Words

▶ **Words That Compare**

When authors compare, they show how two things are alike. Authors use signal words such as *alike, both*, same, *also*, and *too* to compare two things.

Read the passage. **Circle** the words that compare two things.

These turtles are (alike.) They look the same. They both can live in the water and on land. They also have shells on their backs. The shells protect them. These two turtles are good swimmers, too.

My Notes

Read "Gray Wolf! Red Fox!" Use this page to take notes as you read.

_____

_____

_____

_____

_____

_____

_____

_____

_____

_____

_____

_____

GRAY WOLF! RED FOX!

Essential Question

How do animals adapt to challenges in their habitat?

Read how gray wolves and red foxes adapt.

Did you ever see a picture of a gray wolf or a red fox? They look a lot like dogs. Wolves, dogs, and foxes are **related**. They are part of the same family. They look alike, but are different in many ways.

LOOKS ARE EVERYTHING

The gray wolf is the largest member of the wild dog family. The red fox is smaller. Both have **excellent** hearing.

The gray wolf and red fox both have long, **bushy** tails. The wolf's tail can be two feet long. The fox's tail is shorter and has a white tip. Foxes use their thick, shaggy tails as **protection** from the cold.

The gray wolf and red fox are both mammals.

Text Evidence

1 Expand Vocabulary

Reread the third paragraph. Write words that help describe what **bushy** means.

_____

_____

2 Comprehension
Compare and Contrast

Reread the section "Looks Are Everything." **Circle** two ways the gray wolf and red fox are alike.

3 Comprehension
Compare and Contrast

Write one way the gray wolf and red fox are different.

_____

_____

Underline the text evidence.

Text Evidence

1 Organization ⒶⒸⓉ

Look at the map in the sidebar. How many states do both the red fox and gray wolf live in?

_____

2 Expand Vocabulary

Reread the third paragraph. Write a word that means almost the same as **raid**.

_____

3 Comprehension
Compare and Contrast

Reread "Finding Food." **Underline** the ways that red foxes and gray wolves are different. What signal word does the author use?

_____

Foxes and wolves also have thick fur. Red foxes often have red fur. A gray wolf's fur is usually gray and brown.

FINDING FOOD

Gray wolves and red foxes live in many different habitats. They live in forests, deserts, woodlands, and grasslands. But as more people build roads and shopping centers, both animals have lost their homes. The red fox has made changes to fit its **environment**. Many live near towns and parks. Wolves, however, stay far away from people.

Foxes and wolves are not in **competition** for food. Red foxes **prefer** to hunt alone. They eat small animals, birds, and fish. They also **raid**, or rob, garbage cans for food. Wolves work together in packs, or groups. They hunt large animals such as deer.

WHERE DO THEY LIVE?

United States of America

N
W E
S

LEGEND
- Red Fox only
- Gray Wolf only
- Both

Gray wolves prefer to hunt in packs.

DAY-TO-DAY

Wolves live in packs of four to seven. They hunt, travel, and find **shelter** together. Foxes like to live alone. They often sleep in the open or in an empty rabbit hole.

The red fox hunts for food alone.

Both wolves and foxes bark and growl. The gray wolf also howls to **alert**, or warn, other wolves when there is danger. The red fox waves its tail in the air to **caution** other foxes.

The gray wolf and red fox are members of the same family. They have many things in common. But they are two very different animals.

Text Evidence

❶ Comprehension
Compare and Contrast

Reread "Day-to-Day." Write one thing that the gray wolf and red fox have in common.

_____

Underline things that are different about the two animals.

❷ Expand Vocabulary

Reread the second paragraph. **Draw a box** around two words that mean the same as **caution**.

❸ Organization (A)(C)(T)

Reread the third paragraph. Here, the author sums up the information in the text. What information does the author give?

_____

_____

259

Respond to Reading

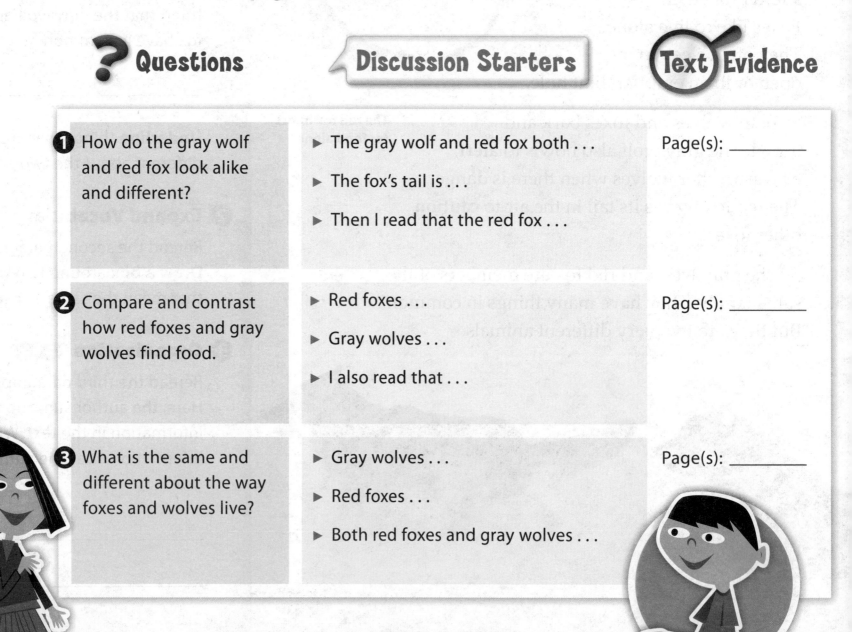

Discuss Work with a partner. Use the discussion starters to answer the questions about "Gray Wolf! Red Fox!" Write the page numbers.

? Questions

Discussion Starters

Text Evidence

1 How do the gray wolf and red fox look alike and different?

▶ The gray wolf and red fox both . . .

▶ The fox's tail is . . .

▶ Then I read that the red fox . . .

Page(s): _____

2 Compare and contrast how red foxes and gray wolves find food.

▶ Red foxes . . .

▶ Gray wolves . . .

▶ I also read that . . .

Page(s): _____

3 What is the same and different about the way foxes and wolves live?

▶ Gray wolves . . .

▶ Red foxes . . .

▶ Both red foxes and gray wolves . . .

Page(s): _____

Mike Moran

260

Write Review your notes. Then use text evidence to support your answer.

How do wolves and foxes adapt to challenges in their habitats?

The gray wolf and red fox both _____

_____

This helps them _____

_____

Foxes find food _____

_____

Wolves find food _____

_____

Both wolves and foxes need to _____

_____

_____

Write About Reading

Shared Read

Student Model

In "Gray Wolf! Red Fox!" the author uses photographs and captions to help me understand how foxes and wolves are the same and different. Photographs help me see how the gray wolf and red fox look different. They also show how the animals look alike. Captions tell more information. The author does a good job using photographs and captions to help me understand more about wolves and foxes.

Topic Sentence

Circle the topic sentence. What does Ray tell?

Evidence

Draw a box around the text evidence. Is there any other evidence in the selection Ray can tell about?

Concluding Statement

Underline the concluding statement. Why is it a good way to end the paragraph?

Leveled Reader

Write an Analysis **Text Features** Write about "Life in a Tide Pool." How well do you think the author uses photographs and captions to give more information about the topic in Chapter 1?

In _____

I think the author uses photographs and captions

to _____

_____

For example, the author uses _____

_____

The author also _____

_____

I think these _____

_____

_____

Topic Sentence

☐ Include the title of the text you read.

Evidence

☐ Tell how the author uses photographs and captions.

☐ Give examples.

Concluding Statement

☐ Restate how the author uses photographs and captions to help the reader.

Talk About It

Essential Question

How are people able to fly?

Go Digital!

264

Write words that tell about different ways people fly.

Flight

Describe one way people fly. Use the words you wrote above.

Vocabulary

 Work with a partner to complete each activity.

1 direction

Jamie blew in the *direction* of the candles and they went out.
Read the sentence above out loud. What does *direction* mean?

_____

_____

2 motion

The *motion*, or movement, of the rollercoaster made Mia feel sick. What word means the same as *motion*?

_____

3 controlled

Dan *controlled* the kite by moving the string left and right. Have you ever *controlled* a toy boat or car? Explain how you got it to go where you wanted.

4 passenger

The *passenger* on a bus can read a book. What are two more things a *passenger* can do?

_____

_____

5 flight

My grandfather's *flight,* or airplane trip, from Maine to New York, was late because of bad weather. What words help you understand what *flight* means?

_____

6 popular

Swimming is a very *popular* activity in the summer. Circle examples of activities that might be *popular* in the winter.

biking   ice skating   skiing   diving

7 **impossible**

The prefix *im-* means "not" or "the opposite of." Underline the root word in *impossible*. What does *impossible* mean?

_____

8 **launched**

Draw a picture of what a rocket looks like when it is *launched* into space.

High-Utility Words

▶ **Words That Compare**

Words with *-er*, such as *stronger* and *slower*, compare two things. Words with *-est*, such as *biggest* and *newest*, compare more than two things.

Read the passage. **Circle** the words that compare two things. **Underline** the words that compare more than two things.

This was the (biggest) festival ever. More than fifty hot air balloons came. Troy's hot air balloon was the largest. It was wider than Jan's and taller than Lucy's. Bill's hot air balloon flew the highest. This was the greatest day!

My Notes

Read "Firsts in Flight." Use this page to take notes as you read.

_____

_____

_____

_____

_____

_____

_____

_____

_____

_____

_____

Firsts in Flight

Essential Question

How are people able to fly?

Read about how inventors learned how to fly.

Orville and Wilbur Wright

Orville and Wilbur Wright stood on a beach in Kitty Hawk, North Carolina. The brothers had traveled a long way from their home in Dayton, Ohio. They wanted to test their newest flying machine.

The Wright brothers owned a bicycle shop. They built new bicycles. They worked on **repairing** bicycles that needed to be fixed. They also built flying machines. They flew their first flying machine in 1899. But the winds were not strong enough to keep it in **motion**. So they looked for a very windy place. As a result, they chose Kitty Hawk. The winds were stronger there.

On December 17, 1903, the *Wright Flyer* flew at Kitty Hawk.

Text Evidence

1 Expand Vocabulary

Reread the second paragraph. **Draw a box** around a word that helps you figure out what **repairing** means.

2 Comprehension
Cause and Effect

Why doesn't the first flying machine stay in motion?

_____

_____

Circle the text evidence.

3 Connection of Ideas A C T

Why do the Wright brothers choose Kitty Hawk to test their flying machine?

_____

Underline the text evidence.

269

Text Evidence

❶ Comprehension
Cause and Effect

Why do the Wright brothers build a better glider?

_____

_____

Circle the signal words.

❷ Expand Vocabulary

Reread the first paragraph. What word helps you figure out what **experimented** means?

_____

_____

❸ Connection of Ideas Ⓐ Ⓒ Ⓣ

Reread the section "Flying Firsts." Was the *Wright Flyer* a success? Explain.

_____

_____

Underline the text evidence.

270

Because their first **flight** was not successful, the Wright brothers learned a lot. As a result, they built a better glider with bigger wings. This glider did not work well either. But they did not give up. The brothers **experimented** with, or tested, a new glider in 1902. Then they built the *Wright Flyer* a year later. It was their first plane with an engine.

Flying Firsts

On December 17, they began testing the *Wright Flyer*. Orville started the engines. He **controlled** the plane, while Wilbur watched from the ground. The *Flyer* was **launched**. It moved in an upward **direction** and flew for twelve seconds. The Wright brothers were successful.

Alberto Santos-Dumont was the first pilot to fly in front of an audience.

The brothers kept making better planes. Soon, other people tried to fly airplanes.

Will It Fly?

Do this experiment with a paper airplane.

Materials needed:

• pencil • paper • ruler

Directions:

1. With a partner, fold two paper airplanes. Make the wing sizes different.

2. Gently throw one plane.

3. Measure how far the plane flew. Write it down.

4. Take turns throwing the plane four more times. Measure and record how far it flies.

5. Repeat with the other airplane.

6. Compare the measurements. Discuss what you learned.

In 1906, one pilot made the first flight in front of an audience. Then, a French pilot flew a plane with a **passenger**.

Better Flying Machines

Because of these two flights, the study of flight became **popular**. Better planes were traveling longer **distances**. They were flying farther and farther. In 1909, a French pilot flew an airplane across the English Channel.

Soon inventors built airplanes that could carry more people. By 1920, passengers were given the chance to fly. Humans had done the **impossible**. They had learned to fly.

This is what an airplane looked like in 1930.

Text Evidence

1 Comprehension
Cause and Effect

What caused the study of flight to become popular?

_____

_____

Circle the signal word.

2 Expand Vocabulary

What words help you understand what **distances** means?

_____

3 Connection of Ideas A C T

Look at the photograph and read the caption. What new information did you learn?

_____

_____

271

(t) Everett Collection/SuperStock; (b) Stockdisc/Getty Images

Respond to Reading

Discuss Work with a partner. Use the discussion starters to answer the questions about "Firsts in Flight." Write the page numbers.

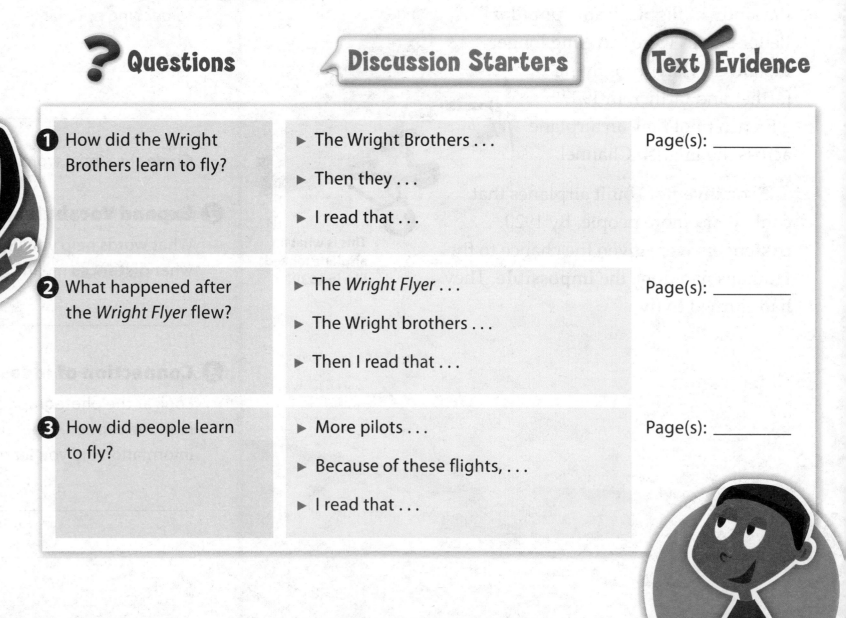

? Questions	Discussion Starters	Text Evidence
1 How did the Wright Brothers learn to fly?	▶ The Wright Brothers . . . ▶ Then they . . . ▶ I read that . . .	Page(s): _____
2 What happened after the *Wright Flyer* flew?	▶ The *Wright Flyer* . . . ▶ The Wright brothers . . . ▶ Then I read that . . .	Page(s): _____
3 How did people learn to fly?	▶ More pilots . . . ▶ Because of these flights, . . . ▶ I read that . . .	Page(s): _____

Mike Moran

Write Review your notes. Then use text evidence to answer the question below.

How were the Wright brothers able to fly?

The Wright brothers _____

_____

_____

They tested _____

_____

Then more pilots _____

_____

_____

Finally, people _____

_____

_____

Write About Reading

Shared Read

Read an Analysis ▶ **Cause and Effect** Read Kelly's paragraph about "Firsts in Flight." She writes her opinion about the author's use of cause and effect.

Student Model

Topic Sentence

Circle the topic sentence. What does Kelly tell?

Evidence

Draw a box around the text evidence. Is there any other evidence in the selection Kelly can tell about?

Concluding Statement

Underline the concluding statement. Why is it a good way to end the paragraph?

In "Firsts in Flight," the author uses causes and effects to show the history of flight in time order. The author writes that first the Wright Brothers tested their flying machine. Their first flights were not always successful. As a result, they learned a lot and built better planes. The author does a good job using causes and effects to show how people learned to fly.

Leveled Reader

Write an Analysis ▶ **Cause and Effect** Write about "The Future of Flight." How do you think the author uses cause and effect to show the events in time order?

In _____

I think the author uses cause and effect to show us

_____

For example, the author says that _____

_____

_____

The author also says that _____

_____

_____

I think the author uses cause and effect to show

_____

_____

Topic Sentence

☐ Include the title of the text you read.

Evidence

☐ Tell how the author uses causes and effect.

☐ Give examples.

Concluding Statement

☐ Restate how the author used cause and effect to help readers understand the events in the selection.

Talk About It

Weekly Concept Inspiration

Essential Question

How can others inspire us?

Go Digital!

276

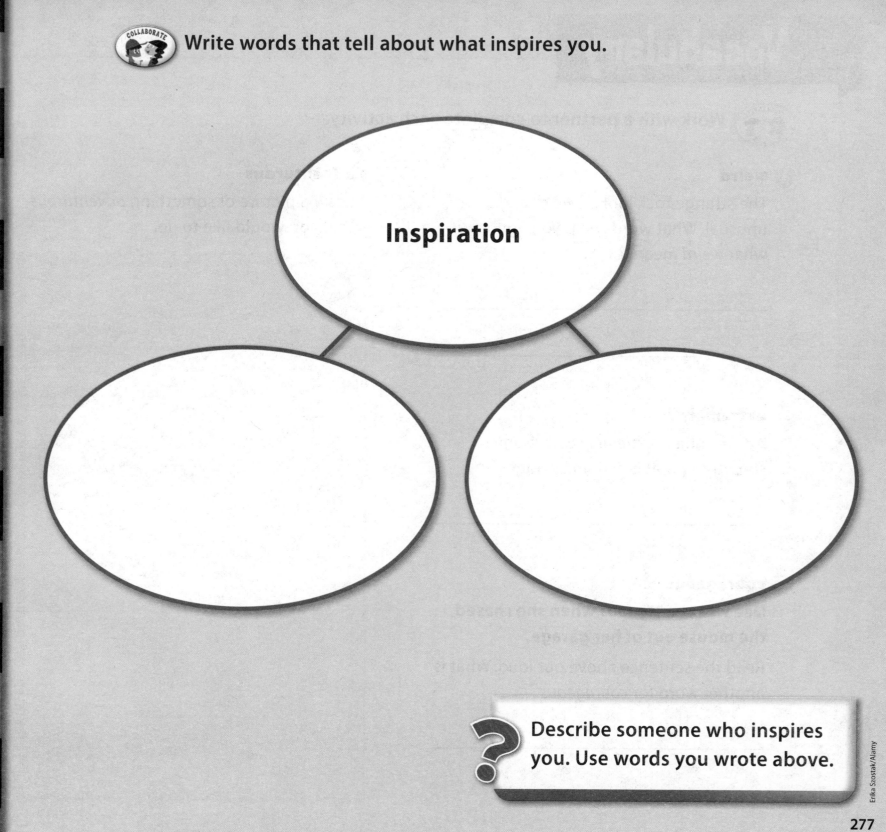

Write words that tell about what inspires you.

Inspiration

Describe someone who inspires you. Use words you wrote above.

Vocabulary

 Work with a partner to complete each activity.

1 weird

The strange rock looked *weird* and unusual. What words help you figure out what *weird* means?

_____

_____

2 extremely

An ice cube is *extremely* cold. Name something that is *extremely* hot.

_____

3 courageous

Dee was *courageous* when she chased the mouse out of her garage.

Read the sentence above out loud. What is another word for *courageous*.

_____

4 adventurous

Draw a picture of something *adventurous* that you would like to do.

Read each poem. Work with a partner to complete each activity.

The Drum

When my sister plays the drum
Her hands are a hummingbird's wings.

When she plays,
Her hands move as fast as a train.

When she plays,
The drumming sounds like rain.

When my sister plays the drum
Her hands move fast, so fast.
She loves to play.
She could play all day.

5 **narrative poem**

What story does this *narrative poem* tell?

_____

_____

6 **repetition**

Reread the poem. Circle two examples of *repetition*.

7 **free verse**

Reread the first stanza. How can you tell this is a *free verse* poem?

_____

_____

8 **rhyme**

Draw a box around two words that *rhyme*.

_____

My Notes

Read the poems. Take notes as you read.

_____

_____

_____

_____

_____

_____

_____

_____

_____

_____

_____

_____

_____

Ginger's Fingers

Ginger's fingers are shooting stars,

They talk of adventurous trips to Mars.

Fingers talking without words,

Signing when sounds can't be heard.

Ginger's fingers are ocean waves,

They talk of fish and deep sea caves.

Fingers talking without words,

Signing when sounds can't be heard.

Ginger's fingers are butterflies,

They talk of a honey-gold sunrise.

Fingers talking without words,

Signing when sounds can't be heard.

Essential Question

How can others inspire us?
Read about different ways
that people inspire others.

The Giant

Dodge, dart, dash,
Zigzag, slash!
I sizzle, SIZZLE, when I dribble,
I'm lightning on the court.
My team calls me The Giant,
Even though I'm kinda short.

The other team might laugh to see
A player tiny as a flea.

But I'm a rocket, fiery hot,
Watch me soar, SOAR, on my jump shot!

Stretching, flexing, push, push, PUSH,
My ball flies up and in—Swoosh Woosh!

I show them all
You don't need to be tall
To rule the ball!

Text Evidence

1 Connection of Ideas Ⓐ Ⓒ Ⓣ

Reread "Ginger's Fingers." What does the poet compare Ginger's fingers to?

_____

_____

2 Comprehension
Theme

Reread "The Giant." **Underline** details that help you figure out the theme of this poem.

3 Comprehension
Theme

Reread the underlined details. Use them to figure out the theme of "The Giant."

_____

_____

Text Evidence

1 Literary Elements
Repetition

Reread the first stanza.
Circle two examples of repetition.

2 Connection of Ideas ⒶⒸⓉ

What is the weather like at the beginning of the poem?

_____

_____

Draw a box around the text evidence.

3 Comprehension
Theme

Underline details that tell about how the weather affects the crew.

Captain's Log,
May 12, 1868

We set sail from a port in Spain,
Sun high, no sign of rain.
The sea was satin, so blue—so blue.
Our ship was a bird, we flew—we flew.

Just past noon, how very weird,
Came a sound that we most feared.
Thunder rumbled, a giant drum.
Thunder rumbled, rum tum tum.

Rain was pouring, pouring.
The wind was a monster, roaring, roaring.
My crew, extremely terrified,
Froze at their posts, pale and wide-eyed.

A huge wave lifted up our ship,
My feet began to slip, slip, slip.
I knew that it was up to me,
To guide us through that stormy sea.

I grabbed a rope, reached for the mast,
And got back to the helm at last—at last
Shook off the rain, looked at my crew,
"Steady lads, I'll get us through."

The crew heard my call,
Each lad stood up tall.
All hands now on deck, we trimmed
    every sail.
Courageous, together, we rode out
    that gale.

Text Evidence

❶ Literary Elements
Narrative Poem

What story does this poem tell?

_____

_____

❷ Comprehension
Theme

Reread the first poem. **Underline** details that tell what the narrator says and does.

❸ Comprehension
Theme

Reread the details about what the narrator says and does. Use them to tell the theme.

_____

_____

Tetra Images/SuperStock

Respond to Reading

COLLABORATE

Discuss ▸ Work with a partner. Use the discussion starters to answer the questions about "The Giant." Write the page numbers.

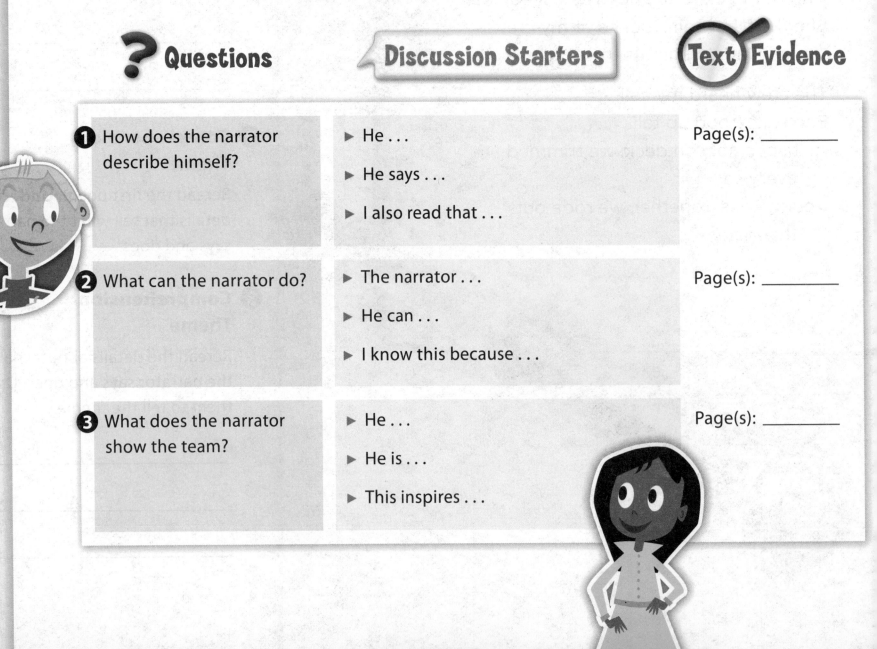

? Questions | **Discussion Starters** | **Text Evidence**

1 How does the narrator describe himself?
- ▸ He . . .
- ▸ He says . . .
- ▸ I also read that . . .

Page(s): _____

2 What can the narrator do?
- ▸ The narrator . . .
- ▸ He can . . .
- ▸ I know this because . . .

Page(s): _____

3 What does the narrator show the team?
- ▸ He . . .
- ▸ He is . . .
- ▸ This inspires . . .

Page(s): _____

Write **Review your notes. Then use text evidence to answer the question below.**

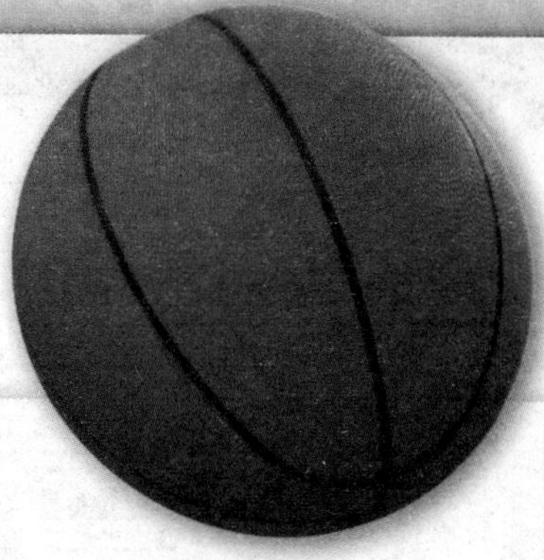

How does the narrator inspire us?

The narrator ______________________________

____

____

His team calls him ______________________________

____

He is really ______________________________

____

____

The narrator is inspiring because ______________________________

____

____

Write About Reading

Shared Read

Read an Analysis **Theme** Read Riley's paragraph below about "Captain's Log, May 12, 1868." She gives her opinion about whether the poet gives enough details to help her figure out the theme.

Student Model

In "Captain's Log, May 12, 1868," the poet gives enough details to help me tell the theme. First I read that the crew set sail on a sunny day. Then, a storm comes and they are scared. The narrator takes charge and is brave. Then they are all brave. The poet gives plenty of details to help me figure out that the theme is about how one brave person can inspire others to be brave, too.

Topic Sentence

Circle the topic sentence. What does Riley tell?

Evidence

Draw a box around the text evidence. Is there any other evidence in the selection Riley can tell about?

Concluding Statement

Underline the concluding statement. Why is it a good way to end the paragraph?

Leveled Reader

Write an Analysis **Theme** Write about "A Speech to Remember." Do you think the author gives enough details to show the theme in Chapter 1?

In _____

the author tells about _____

_____

For example, the author says that _____

_____

_____

The author also says that _____

_____

_____

These details support _____

_____

_____

Topic Sentence

☐ Include the title of the text you read.

Evidence

☐ Tell whether the author gives enough details to tell the theme of the story.

☐ Give examples.

Concluding Statement

☐ Restate how the author uses enough details to tell the theme.

UNIT
5

TAKE ACTION

THE BIG IDEA

What are ways people can take action?

Talk About It

Weekly Concept Let's Trade

Essential Question

How do we get what we need?

Go Digital!

How do we get what we need?

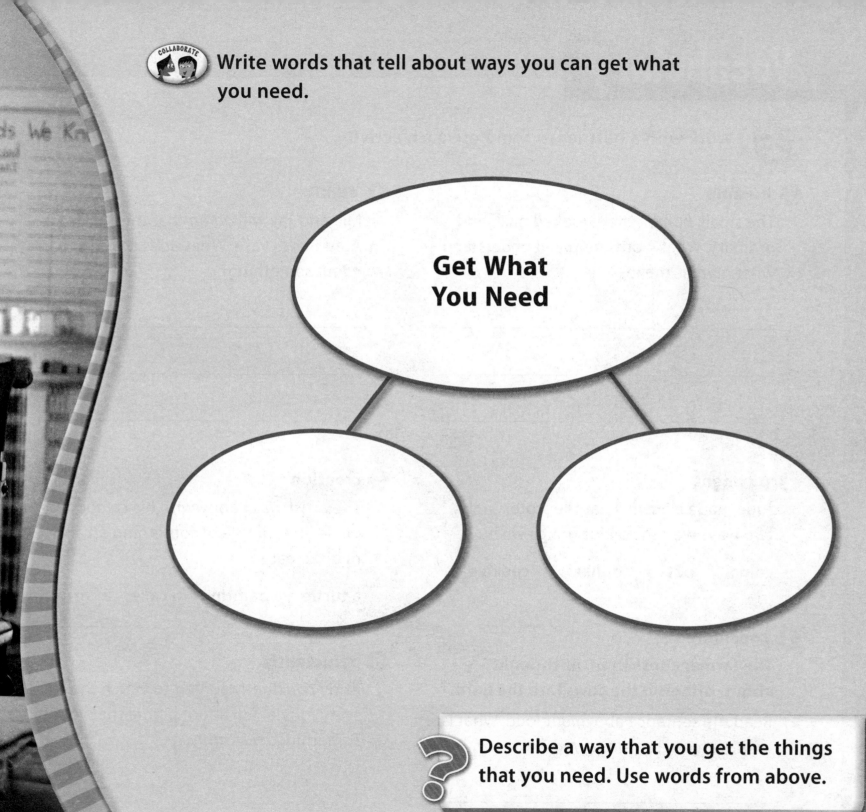

COLLABORATE

Write words that tell about ways you can get what you need.

Get What
You Need

Describe a way that you get the things that you need. Use words from above.

Vocabulary

 Work with a partner to complete each activity.

1 humble

The small, *humble* store looked plain and ordinary. What words help you understand what *humble* means?

_____

_____

2 payment

June made a *payment* at the store. Circle two ways we can pay for things we buy.

coins   pets   dollars   cookies

3 considered

The farmer *considered*, or thought about, bringing the cows into the barn.

Read the sentence above out loud. What is another word for *considered*?

_____

4 admit

Mia and Jay will *admit* that they broke Aunt Barb's vase. What does it mean to *admit* something?

_____

_____

5 creation

The artist was happy with his *creation*. Circle an example of something an artist might create.

a turtle   a painting   a cake   a carrot

6 reluctantly

Andy *reluctantly* agreed to watch the scary movie. Tell about a time that you did something *reluctantly*.

292

7 **barter**

Jerry wants to *barter*, or trade, with May. What word means almost the same as *barter*?

_____

8 **magnificent**

Draw something in nature that you think is *magnificent*.

▶ **Singular Possessives**

A **possessive noun** is a noun that shows who or what owns or has something. Add an **apostrophe (') + s** to a singular noun to make it possessive.

Read the passage. **Circle** the singular possessive nouns.

There once was a girl. She liked to visit her (grandma's) farm. The girl's dog went, too. They fed the horses. They collected the hen's eggs. Grandma's tractor is red. The tractor's engine roars. The farm is the girl's favorite place.

McGraw-Hill Education/Steve Mack

Read "Juanita and the Beanstalk." Use this page to take notes as you read.

_____

_____

_____

_____

_____

_____

_____

_____

_____

_____

Shared Read Genre • Fairy Tale

Juanita and the Beanstalk

? Essential Question

How do we get what we need?

Read about what Juanita does to get what she needs.

Chris Vallo

Juanita lived in a small, **humble** home with her Mamá and pet goat, Pepe.

One day Mamá said, "There has been no rain, and our garden is dry. Juanita, you must go to town and sell your goat. Use the money as **payment** to buy food."

"I don't want to sell Pepe!" cried Juanita. She petted her goat lovingly. But she always did what she was asked and would not **disobey** her mother. She **reluctantly** took Pepe to town. On her way, she met an old man who patted Pepe kindly.

"He is for sale," said Juanita with tears in her eyes.

"I have no money," said the man. "But I do have special *frijoles*. Plant these beans and you will never go hungry. We can **barter**. I will trade the beans for your goat."

Text Evidence

1 **Connection of Ideas** Ⓐ Ⓒ Ⓣ

What is Mamá and Juanita's problem?

_____

_____

Circle the text evidence.

2 **Expand Vocabulary**

Reread the third paragraph. What words help you understand what **disobey** means?

_____

_____

3 **Comprehension**
Point of View

Reread the page. **Underline** details that show what Juanita thinks about Pepe.

295

Text Evidence

1 Expand Vocabulary

An **offer** is a deal or agreement. What does Juanita do about the man's *offer*?

_____

_____

2 Comprehension
Point of View

Reread the first paragraph. What does Juanita think about the man?

_____

_____

Underline the text evidence.

3 Comprehension
Point of View

Reread the third paragraph. How has Juanita's point of view about the trade changed?

Juanita thought carefully and **considered** the man's **offer**. He seemed caring. She thought he would be kind to Pepe, so she took the beans.

At home, Mamá was upset. "We have no food and no money!" she exclaimed.

Juanita had to **admit** that Mamá was right. She only had three beans, and she still missed Pepe. Worst of all, Mamá was unhappy.

Juanita planted the beans and went to bed. The next morning, she went outside. A giant beanstalk reached high into the clouds.

Juanita was curious, so she climbed the beanstalk. At the top, she saw a grand and **magnificent** palace. She knocked on the door, and a maid answered.

"Hide," cried the maid. "The giant dislikes strangers." So Juanita crawled under the table.

Chris Vallo

The giant stomped in carrying an unhappy hen in a cage. "Lay, hen, lay!" he said. Juanita peeked from under the table and breathed in quickly. She **gasped** when saw the hen's **creation**. It was a golden egg!

The poor hen reminded Juanita of Pepe. She ran between the giant's legs and grabbed the hen. The giant roared and chased Juanita. She slid down the beanstalk, but the giant was too heavy. He broke the stalk and it crashed to the ground. Juanita and the hen were safe.

The hen was happy and laid many golden eggs. Mamá was happy to use the eggs to buy food. And Juanita was happy to trade a golden egg to get Pepe back!

Text Evidence

1 Expand Vocabulary

Draw a box around the words that help you understand what **gasped** means.

2 Connection of Ideas (A)(C)(T)

Reread the second paragraph. Why does Juanita save the hen?

_____

_____

_____

3 Comprehension
Point of View

What does Juanita think of Pepe at the end of the story?

_____

_____

Underline text evidence to support your idea.

297

Respond to Reading

Discuss Work with a partner. Use the discussion starters to answer the questions about "Juanita and the Beanstalk." Write the page numbers.

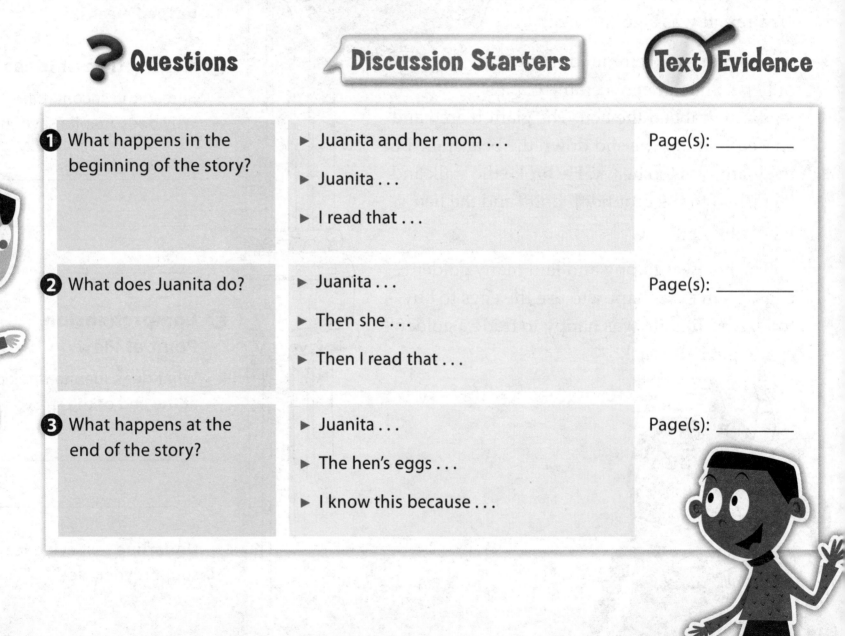

? Questions	Discussion Starters	Text Evidence
1 What happens in the beginning of the story?	▶ Juanita and her mom . . . ▶ Juanita . . . ▶ I read that . . .	Page(s): _____
2 What does Juanita do?	▶ Juanita . . . ▶ Then she . . . ▶ Then I read that . . .	Page(s): _____
3 What happens at the end of the story?	▶ Juanita . . . ▶ The hen's eggs . . . ▶ I know this because . . .	Page(s): _____

Write Review your notes. Then use text evidence to answer the question below.

How does Juanita get what she needs?

Juanita and Mamá _____

_____

_____

Juanita trades _____

_____

Then she _____

_____

_____

At the end of the story, Juanita _____

_____

_____

Write About Reading

Shared Read

Read an Analysis **Point of View** Read Henry's paragraph about "Juanita and the Beanstalk." He analyzes how the author uses what Juanita says and does to show her point of view.

Student Model

In "Juanita and the Beanstalk," the author gives many details about what Juanita thinks about Pepe. First, Juanita does not want to trade Pepe for beans. But she and Mamá need food. She thinks the man will be kind to Pepe. She trades but misses Pepe. The author's details tell how much Juanita loves Pepe.

Topic Sentence

Circle the topic sentence. What does Henry tell?

Evidence

Draw a box around the text evidence. Is there any other evidence in the selection Henry can tell about?

Concluding Statement

Underline the concluding statement. Why is it a good way to end the paragraph?

Leveled Reader

In _____

the author uses details to show _____

_____

For example, the author says that _____

_____

_____

The author also says that _____

_____

_____

These details show _____

_____

_____

Topic Sentence

☐ Include the title of the text you read.

Evidence

☐ Tell how the author uses details to show one character's point of view.

☐ Give examples.

Concluding Statement

☐ Restate how the author shows the character's point of view using details.

Essential Question

How can we reuse what we already have?

Go Digital!

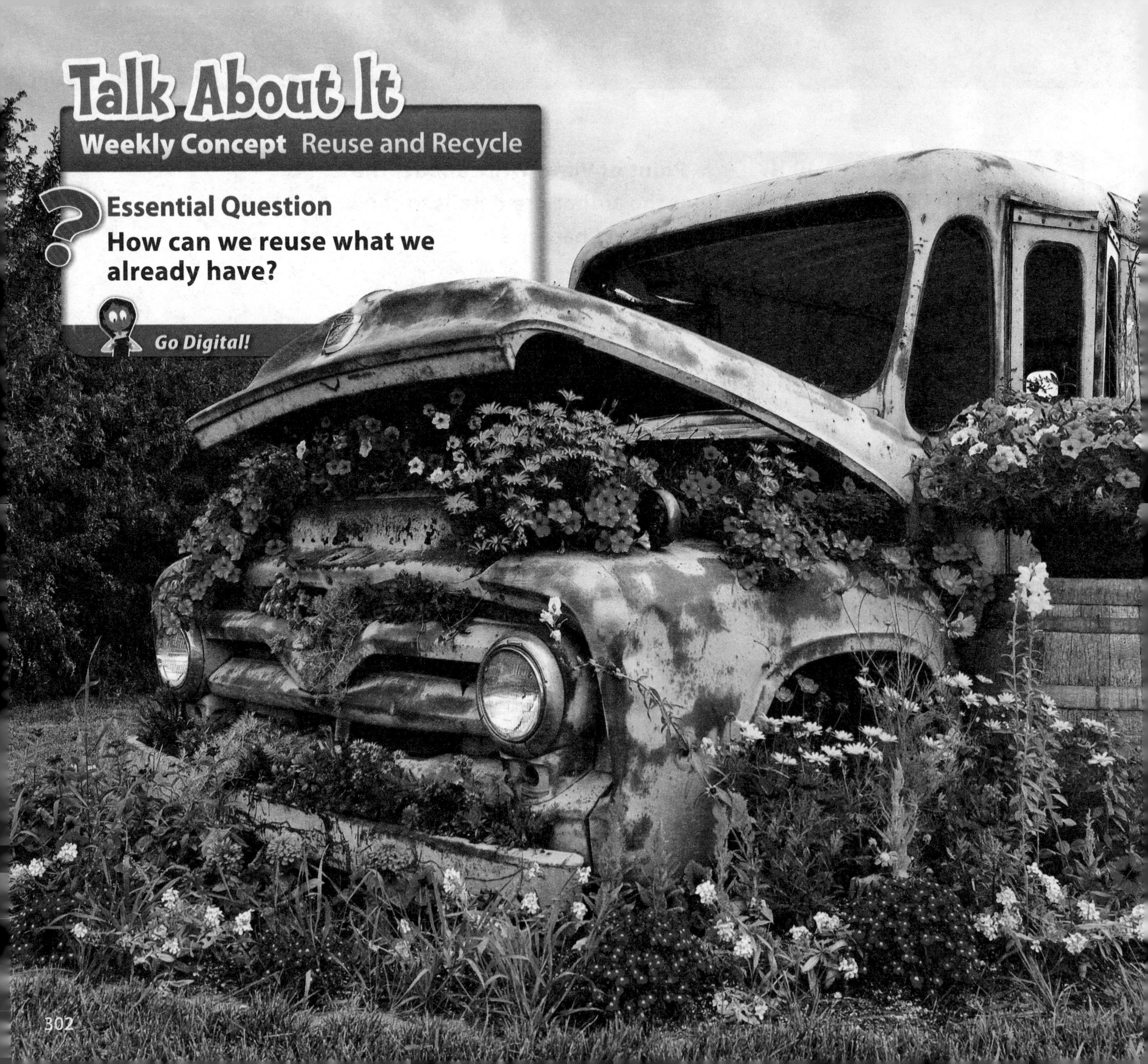

Write words that tell why it is important to reuse things.

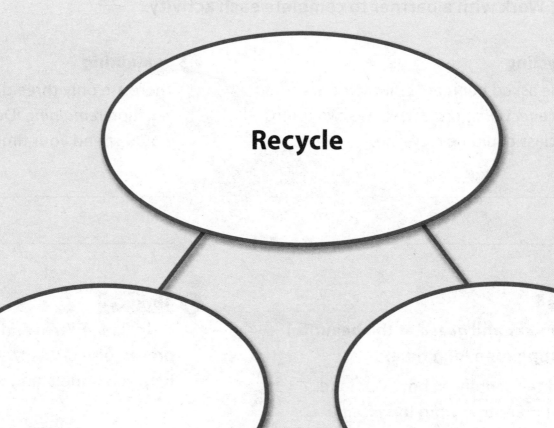

Recycle

 Describe something you have reused. Use words you wrote above.

Vocabulary

1 recycling

Reese asked her teacher if their class could start a *recycling* project. Name two things her class could be *recycling*.

_____

_____

2 gazed

Penny sat and *gazed* at the beautiful painting for a long time.

Read the sentence above out loud. What is another word for *gazed*?

_____

3 discouraged

Emma felt *discouraged* and disappointed when her class trip was cancelled. What word is a synonym for *discouraged*?

_____

4 remaining

There are only three days of summer vacation *remaining*. Describe how you would spend your time.

_____

_____

5 tinkered

Ted's dad *tinkered* and worked on the broken bike until it was fixed. What words help you understand what *tinkered* means?

_____

_____

6 conservation

Denise asked her family to practice *conservation* by using less water at home. Describe a way you can practice *conservation* at home.

7 **frustration**

Neil felt *frustration* when he could not solve the math problem. Act out how Neil might have shown his *frustration*.

8 **jubilant**

Draw something that makes you feel *jubilant*.

High-Utility Words

▶ **Homographs**

Homographs are words that are spelled the same but have different meanings. Use nearby words as clues to help you figure out their meanings.

Read the passage. **Circle** these homographs *can, fair, post, fine.*

Zoe's dad (can) make a hat out of newspaper. He is fair and makes one for her brother, too. Zoe will post a picture so her friends can see it. She thinks it is fine. She will wear it when they go to the fair.

Use context clues. Talk with a partner about what each homograph means.

Read "The New Hoop." Use this page to take notes as you read.

_____

_____

_____

_____

_____

_____

_____

_____

_____

_____

_____

The New HOOP

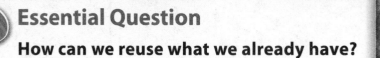

Essential Question

How can we reuse what we already have?

Read to see how Kim and Marco reuse something to solve a problem.

Chris Vallo

Marco **gazed** long and hard at the basketball hoop. He threw the ball up and it fell through the net. "Score!" he shouted.

"I wish we could play at home," said Kim. "I'm tired of playing only at school. It's not fair." The basketball hoop in their park was crushed when a tree fell on it.

"My dad says the town doesn't have enough money to buy a new hoop," grumbled Marco in **frustration**.

"I feel so **discouraged**," said Kim. "I guess there's nothing we can do."

Marco and Kim walked past the city's **recycling** center. They waved to Mr. Morse. His job was to separate the plastic, paper, and metal items. He was taking items from an **overflowing** bin and moving them into large, empty boxes.

Text Evidence

❶ Sentence Structure ACT

Reread the second paragraph. What does Kim say about playing basketball at school?

_____

_____

Circle the text evidence.

❷ Comprehension
Point of View

Reread the fourth paragraph. **Underline** what Kim thinks about not having a basketball hoop at home.

❸ Expand Vocabulary

Reread the last paragraph. What does **overflowing** mean?

_____

_____

Text Evidence

1 **Comprehension**
Point of View

What does Kim think about reusing the plastic basket at first? **Underline** the sentences that tell what she thinks.

2 **Expand Vocabulary**

Reread the last paragraph. A **leftover** is something that is extra or not needed. **Circle** words that help you understand what *leftover* means.

3 **Comprehension**
Point of View

Reread the page. What does Marco think about recycling?

_____

_____

Underline the text evidence.

Marco had an idea. "Mr. Morse, do you have anything we could reuse to make a basketball hoop?"

Mr. Morse picked up an old plastic basket. "Maybe you can use this," he said.

"It looks old and useless," said Kim.

"We can cut off the bottom," said Marco. "It would make a fine hoop."

Kim frowned. "I want a new basketball hoop," she said. "Not someone else's hand-me-down."

"When we reuse things, we practice **conservation**," said Marco. "It stops waste."

"We can try," said Kim. "But I still think a new hoop would be better."

At home, Marco's older brother, Victor, got some **leftover**, unused wood from an old project. They **tinkered** with the wood and made a post and a backboard.

Chris Vallo

When Marco went to get the basket, he found his cats napping in it. "That's another way to reuse the basket!" he laughed.

Everything was ready. There was only one thing **remaining** to do. Marco, Kim, and Victor dug a hole and put the post in the ground.

"It looks better than I thought it would," said Kim.

"Here's the real test!" said Marco. He tossed the ball to Kim. She pointed at the hoop and **aimed** the ball. She shot a perfect basket and was **jubilant**.

"This recycled hoop works great!" she said. "Now we can play whenever we want!"

"And I can beat you whenever I want!" said Marco.

"Oh, no you can't" laughed Kim. The two friends played until dinner time.

Text Evidence

1 Sentence Structure A C T

Reread the fourth paragraph. What does Marco mean when he says, "Here's the real test!"?

_____

_____

Circle the text evidence.

2 Expand Vocabulary

What does **aimed** mean? **Draw a box** around words that help you figure it out.

3 Comprehension
Point of View

What does Kim think about recycling at the end of story?

_____

_____

Underline the text evidence.

Respond to Reading

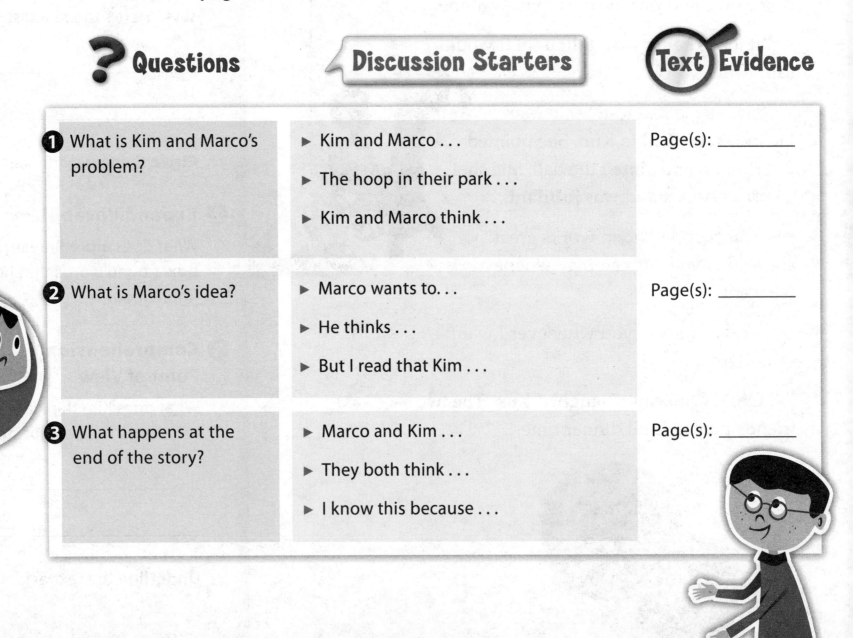

COLLABORATE

Discuss Work with a partner. Use the discussion starters to answer the questions about "The New Hoop." Write the page numbers.

? Questions

Discussion Starters

Text Evidence

1 What is Kim and Marco's problem?
- ▶ Kim and Marco . . .
- ▶ The hoop in their park . . .
- ▶ Kim and Marco think . . .

Page(s): _____

2 What is Marco's idea?
- ▶ Marco wants to. . .
- ▶ He thinks . . .
- ▶ But I read that Kim . . .

Page(s): _____

3 What happens at the end of the story?
- ▶ Marco and Kim . . .
- ▶ They both think . . .
- ▶ I know this because . . .

Page(s): _____

Mike Moran

310

Review your notes. Then use text evidence to answer the question below.

How do Marco and Kim reuse something they already had?

Kim and Marco _____

_____

_____

Marco's idea is to _____

_____

They reuse _____

_____

_____

At the end of the story, Kim and Marco _____

_____

_____

Write About Reading

Shared Read

Student Model

In "The New Hoop," the author gives enough details about what Marco says and does to help me figure out that he thinks recycling is a good idea. At the beginning, Marco and Kim need a new hoop. Marco wants to reuse a plastic basket. He says it will make a fine hoop. It works. The author gives enough details to help me figure out that Marco likes to reuse old things to make new things.

Topic Sentence

Circle the topic sentence. What does Maria tell?

Evidence

Draw a box around the text evidence. Is there any other evidence in the selection Maria can tell about?

Concluding Statement

Underline the concluding statement. Why is it a good way to end the paragraph?

Chris Vallo

Leveled Reader

Write an Analysis ▸ **Point of View** Write about "The Great Book Swap." Do you think the author gives enough details to figure out point of view in Chapter 1?

In _____

_____

I think the author _____

_____

_____

For example, the author says that _____

_____

The author also says that _____

_____

I think the author _____

_____

_____

Topic Sentence

☐ Include the title of the text you read.

Evidence

☐ Tell how the author gives details to show a character's point of view.

☐ Give examples.

Concluding Statement

☐ Restate how the author gives details to show point of view.

313

Talk About It

?

Essential Question
How do teams work together?

Go Digital!

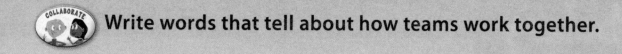 **Write words that tell about how teams work together.**

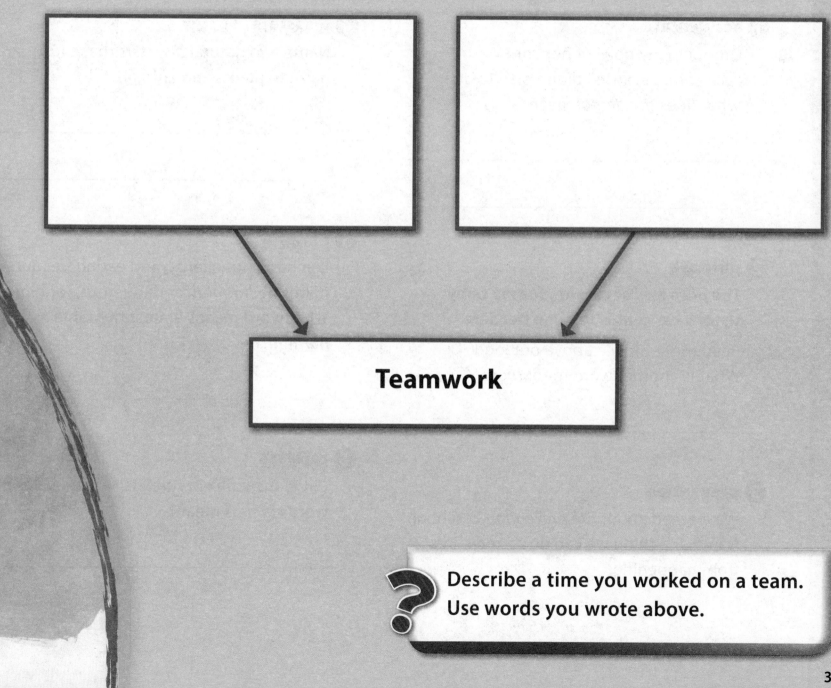

Teamwork

Describe a time you worked on a team. Use words you wrote above.

BLOOM image/Getty Images

315

Vocabulary

 Work with a partner to complete each activity.

1 accidental

Dropping my bowl of popcorn was *accidental* because I didn't plan to do it. What does *accidental* mean?

_____

_____

2 purpose

The *purpose*, or reason, for my baby sister's car seat is to keep her safe.

Read the sentence above out loud. What is another word for *purpose*?

_____

3 prevention

We learned about fire *prevention* at school. Name one thing we can do to keep fires from happening.

4 disasters

Name two natural *disasters* that cause harm to plants and animals.

_____

_____

5 harmful

Len has a nut allergy, and eating peanuts might be *harmful*, or dangerous, for him. What word means almost the same as *harmful*?

_____

6 careless

Circle the suffix in *careless*. What does the word *careless* mean?

_____

7 respond

How do you *respond* to a loud noise?
Act it out.

8 equipment

Draw a picture of a piece of *equipment* a
firefighter might use.

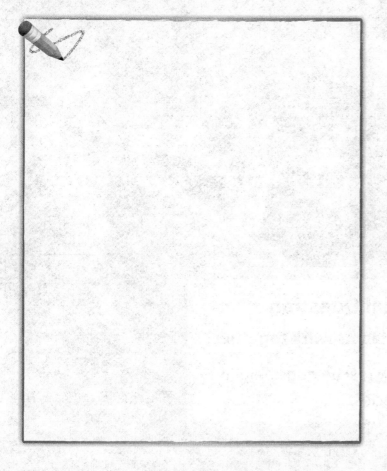

High-Utility Words

▶ **Homophones**

Homophones are words that sound the
same but have different meanings and
different spellings. The words *for* and *four*
are homophones.

Read the passage. **Circle** the
homophones. **Use context clues to
talk about their meanings.**

(There) is a big tree. Abe and
Ana want to build a tree house in its
branches. Abe draws plans for the
house. Ana asks their two friends to
help. Abe's dad will help, too. The four
friends will have fun. It's going to be
a great tree house.

Read "Rescue Dogs Save the Day." Use this page to take notes as you read.

_____

_____

_____

_____

_____

_____

_____

_____

_____

_____

_____

Rescue Dogs Save the Day

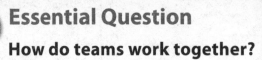

Essential Question

How do teams work together?

Read how rescue dogs help in emergencies.

Rescue dogs go anywhere they are needed.

Frank Leonhardt/dpa picture alliance archive/Alamy Stock Photo

Rescue teams are there when we need them. They **respond** quickly to help people in trouble. They are brave heroes. But heroes aren't always people. Heroes can be dogs, too!

Rescue Dogs Are Heroes

Rescue dogs work with police, fire, and other rescue workers. They help find people who are lost and rescue families after **disasters**. Rescue dogs can do their jobs with no special **equipment**. They only need their excellent hearing and a good nose!

Rescue dogs are smart and brave. They listen well and work even when they are tired, thirsty, or hungry. They are friendly and get along with the people who work with them. They also must be obedient and do what they are told.

One breed that makes a great rescue dog is the Border Collie. Border Collies do not get tired easily. This is important. They also need to follow **commands**. Learning to do what they are told takes a lot of training.

Text Evidence

① **Comprehension**
Author's Point of View

Reread the first three paragraphs. **Underline** details that tell you what the author thinks about rescue dogs.

② **Comprehension**
Author's Point of View

Reread the fourth paragraph. Why do Border Collies make great rescue dogs?

_____

_____

③ **Expand Vocabulary**

Reread the fourth paragraph. **Draw a box** around the words that help you understand what **commands** means.

Text Evidence

1 Expand Vocabulary

Reread the second paragraph. What does it mean to **ignore** something?

_____

_____

2 Organization (A C T)

Reread "Getting Ready to Work." **Circle** three details that tell what rescue dogs must learn to do.

3 Organization (A C T)

Look at the chart. Which dog makes a great rescue dog because it has a great sense of smell?

_____

Circle the text evidence.

Getting Ready to Work

Rescue dogs begin their training as puppies. It can take up to two years to train a rescue dog. Then it is able to save people in **harmful** situations.

The dogs learn to work in heat, cold, and bad weather. They run, jump, and climb for hours every day. Rescue dogs also learn to **ignore**, or pay no attention to, everything around them. This helps them focus on the job. It keeps them from making **careless** mistakes.

Everything a rescue dog learns to do has a **purpose**. Even friendship is not **accidental**. A dog and a rescue worker must learn to communicate. They trust each other. Then, after they have trained enough, the dog can go on a real rescue mission.

Rescue dogs are ready to dive in and help someone.

Best Rescue Dogs

These dogs make great rescue dogs.				
Dog Breed	**Labrador Retriever**	**German Shepherd**	**Bloodhound**	**Border Collie**
Rescue Trait	friendly	brave	great sense of smell	lots of energy

Good Dog!

A dog's sense of smell is very strong. Rescue dogs use this to find lost hikers. When a dog finds someone, it barks to alert its partner. The rescue worker trusts the dog, so the team works quickly to save a life. After every rescue, the dog gets **praise** and treats for doing a great job.

Sometimes rescue teams go to schools. They teach children about safety and disaster **prevention**. This job is fun for rescue dogs. They get lots of attention for helping people. Rescue dogs really are heroes!

This team works on snowy mountains.

Tom Bear/Aurora/Getty Images

Text Evidence

1 Expand Vocabulary

What words help you understand what **praise** means?

_____

_____

2 Comprehension
Author's Point of View

Reread the second paragraph. What does the author think about rescue dogs?

_____

_____

Underline the text evidence.

3 Organization Ⓐ Ⓒ Ⓣ

Reread the caption. What kind of dog is in the photograph? Use the chart on page 320.

_____

321

Respond to Reading

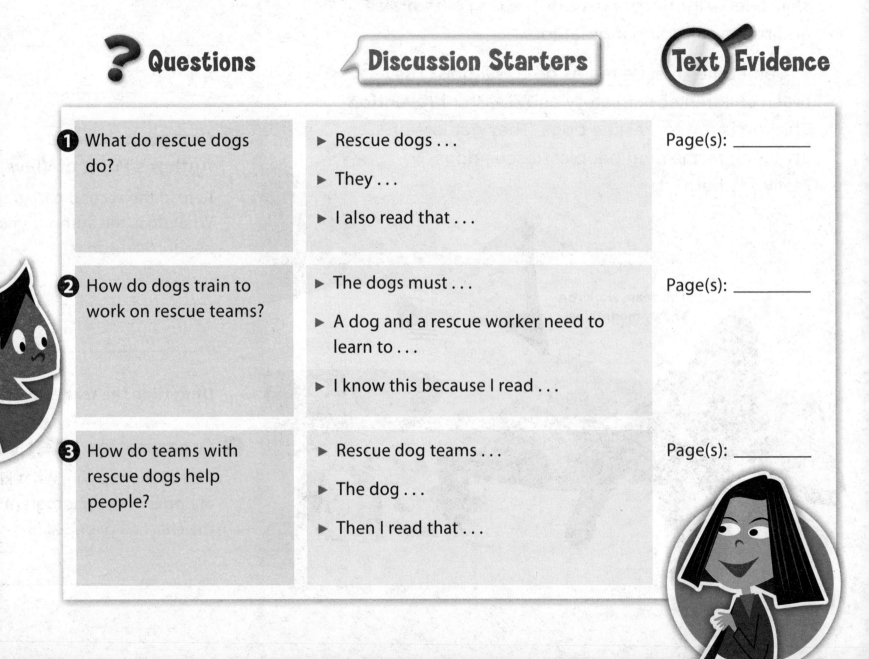

Discuss Work with a partner. Use the discussion starters to answer the questions about "Rescue Dogs Save the Day." Write the page numbers.

COLLABORATE

? Questions	Discussion Starters	Text Evidence
1 What do rescue dogs do?	▶ Rescue dogs . . . ▶ They . . . ▶ I also read that . . .	Page(s): _____
2 How do dogs train to work on rescue teams?	▶ The dogs must . . . ▶ A dog and a rescue worker need to learn to . . . ▶ I know this because I read . . .	Page(s): _____
3 How do teams with rescue dogs help people?	▶ Rescue dog teams . . . ▶ The dog . . . ▶ Then I read that . . .	Page(s): _____

Review your notes. Then use text evidence to answer the question below.

How do rescue dogs and people work together?

Rescue dogs _____

_____

_____

They learn how to _____

_____

Rescue dogs and people work together to _____

_____

_____

Rescue dogs are heroes because _____

_____

_____

Write About Reading

Shared Read

Read an Analysis **Author's Point of View** Read Ben's paragraph about "Rescue Dogs Save the Day." He analyzes how the author uses details to support his point of view. Ben shares his opinion, too.

Student Model

Topic Sentence

Circle the topic sentence. What does Ben tell?

Evidence

Draw a box around the text evidence. Is there any other evidence in the selection Ben can tell about?

Concluding Statement

Underline the concluding statement. Why is it a good way to end the paragraph?

In "Rescue Dogs Save the Day," the author uses details to show that he thinks rescue dogs are heroes. The author explains that rescue dogs are smart and brave. They work even when they are tired or hungry. Rescue dogs help find and rescue people who are lost. There are many details that show what the author thinks. I agree. Rescue dogs really are heroes.

Leveled Reader

Write an Analysis **Point of View** Write about "Firefighting Heroes." How do details show the author's point of view in Chapter 1?

In _____

the author gives details to _____

_____

For example, the author says that _____

_____

_____

The author also says that _____

_____

_____

These details show _____

_____

_____

Topic Sentence

☐ Include the title of the text you read.

Evidence

☐ Tell how the author gives details to show her point of view.

☐ Give examples.

Concluding Statement

☐ Restate how the author gives details to show her point of view.

Talk About It

Weekly Concept Good Citizens

Essential Question

What do good citizens do?

Go Digital!

326

COLLABORATE Write words that tell what good citizens do.

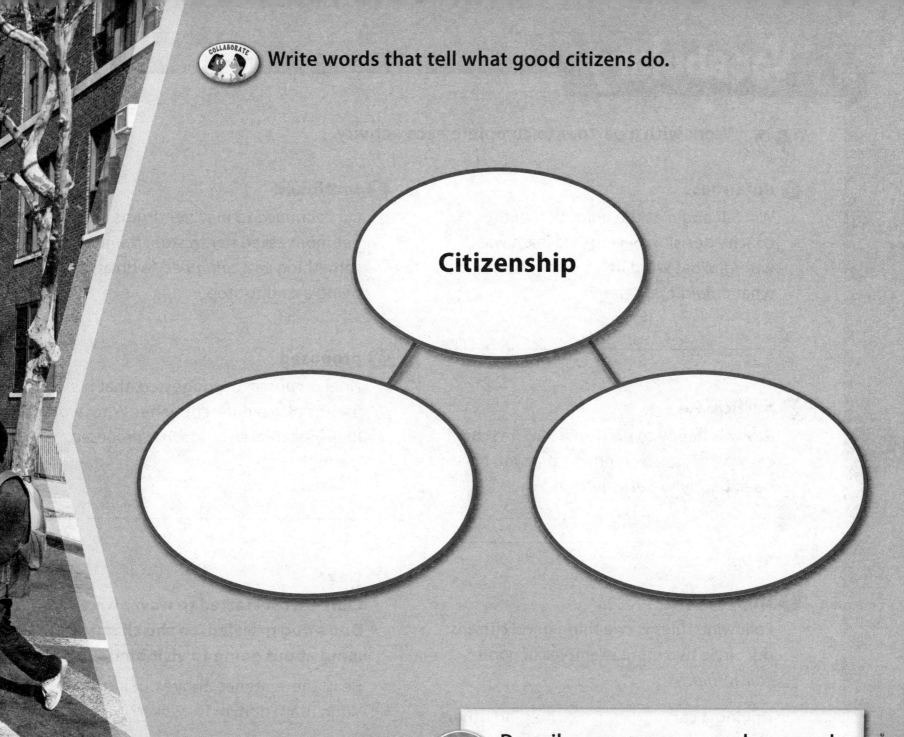

Citizenship

Describe one way you can be a good citizen. Use words from above.

Vocabulary

 Work with a partner to complete each activity.

1 unfairness

Will felt anger at the *unfairness* of the coach's decision because he felt it was wrong. What word helps you understand what *unfairness* means?

_____

2 participate

Ray was happy to *participate* in the school car wash. Name something that you have been happy to *participate* in.

_____

3 citizenship

Following rules is one thing good citizens do. Circle two more examples of good *citizenship*.

driving a car   helping others

being respectful   playing games

4 continued

Lin *continued* to play her drums after her mom asked her to stop. Name something you *continued* to do after being asked to stop.

5 proposed

Noel *proposed*, or suggested, that his friends play a different game. What word helps you understand what *proposed* means?

_____

6 waver

Clare's trust started to *waver* when Don's dog growled, so she changed her mind about going to visit him.

Read the sentence above out loud. What is a synonym for *waver*?

_____

7 **horrified**

Tony was *horrified* when he found out the math test was today. Show how you would look if you were *horrified*.

8 **daring**

Draw a picture of a *daring* activity that you might need courage to do.

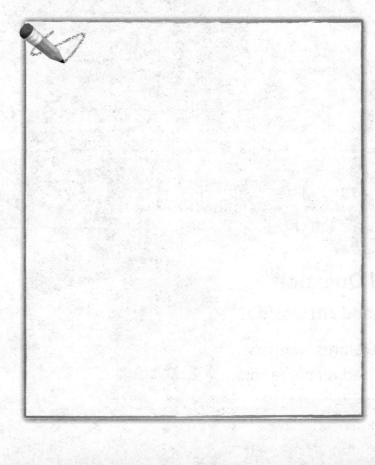

High-Utility Words

▶ **Prefixes**

A prefix is a word part added to the beginning of a word. It changes the meaning of the word. The prefixes *un-* and *dis-* mean "not."

Read the passage. **Circle** words with *un-* and *dis-*. Talk about their meanings.

Maria and Mark (dislike) seeing trash in the park. They want it to disappear.

"It is unsafe to play there," said Mark.

"It's unfair to the kids in the community," said Maria.

Maria and Mark talk to the mayor. They make a plan. Soon the unclean mess is gone.

My Notes

Read "Dolores Huerta: Growing Up Strong." Use this page to take notes as you read.

_____

_____

_____

_____

_____

_____

_____

_____

_____

_____

_____

_____

Dolores Huerta
GROWING UP STRONG

Essential Question

What do good citizens do?

Read how Dolores Huerta's actions helped many people.

Dolores Huerta learned to help people by watching her mother. Good **citizenship** was important to her. She taught Dolores that women can be strong leaders.

Good Citizens

Dolores was born in New Mexico. When she was three years old, she moved to California with her mother and two brothers. Dolores watched her mother **participate**, or join, in community groups. Her mother believed that all people should be treated fairly.

When Dolores was young, her mother owned a hotel and a **restaurant**. Many farm workers in their town were poor and hungry. They worked hard and were paid very little. Dolores' mother let them stay at her hotel. She let them eat at her restaurant for free. Dolores learned that good citizens help their neighbors.

Farm workers spent many hours working in fields.

Dr. Parvinder Sethi

Text Evidence

1 Expand Vocabulary

Reread the third paragraph. What words help you understand what a **restaurant** is?

_____

_____

2 Comprehension
Author's Point of View

Reread the page. **Circle** the details that tell about Dolores Huerta's mother.

3 Genre A C T

Look at the photograph and reread the caption. What new detail does the caption tell?

_____

_____

Text Evidence

1 Expand Vocabulary

Reread the first paragraph. What does the word **attitude** mean?

_____

_____

Underline the text evidence.

2 Comprehension
Author's Point of View

Reread the page. **Circle** the details that tell what the author thinks about Dolores. What is the author's point of view?

_____

_____

_____

3 Genre Ⓐ🅒Ⓣ

Look at the time line. When does Dolores meet César Chávez?

_____

Dolores Goes to School

Dolores saw how hard life was for farm workers. She wanted everyone to be treated fairly. Her **attitude**, or way of thinking, **continued** as she attended college. She studied to become a teacher.

Many of the students that Dolores taught were the children of farm workers. These students were often tired and hungry. Many of them had no shoes. Dolores wanted to help. So she went to the school's principal and **proposed** some good ideas. She tried to get free lunches and milk for the children. She tried to get them new clothes and shoes.

Trying to help the children was a **daring** thing for Dolores to do. Other teachers disagreed with her ideas, but her beliefs did not **waver**. She wanted to do something about the **unfairness** she saw.

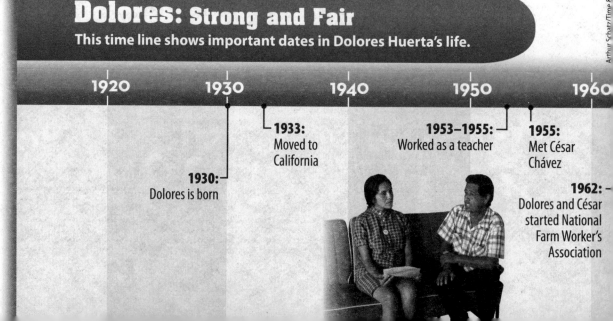

Dolores: Strong and Fair
This time line shows important dates in Dolores Huerta's life.

1920   1930   1940   1950   1960

1930: Dolores is born

1933: Moved to California

1953–1955: Worked as a teacher

1955: Met César Chávez

1962: Dolores and César started National Farm Worker's Association

Arthur Schatz/Time & Life Pictures/Getty Images

Dolores Stands Strong

Dolores saw people working in unsafe and disagreeable places. She was **horrified**. Many farm workers had little money to feed their families. Dolores decided to do something.

In 1955, Dolores met César Chávez. He wanted to help farm workers, too. They **organized**, or got the workers together into, a group called the National Farm Workers Association. This group protected the rights of the farm workers. It made big farms treat them better.

Growing up with a mother who cared about other people taught Dolores to be a good citizen. Her kind and brave acts helped farm workers and their families. Who is a good citizen? Dolores Huerta is!

Dolores Huerta speaks for farm workers at a rally in 1969.

1970   1980   1990   2000   2010

1975: Helped pass laws to protect farm workers

1998: Earned Human Rights Award from President Clinton

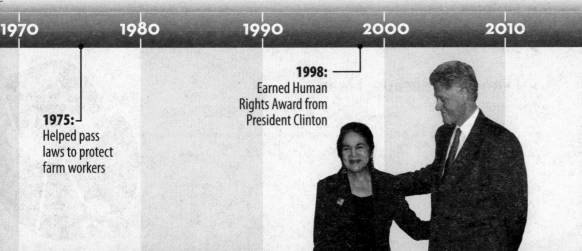

Text Evidence

① Genre A C T

Reread the caption. What new information do you learn about Dolores?

_____

_____

② Expand Vocabulary

Reread the second paragraph. **Underline** the words help you understand what **organized** means.

③ Comprehension
Author's Point of View

Circle details that show what the author thinks about Dolores. What is the author's point of view of Dolores Huerta?

_____

_____

333

Respond to Reading

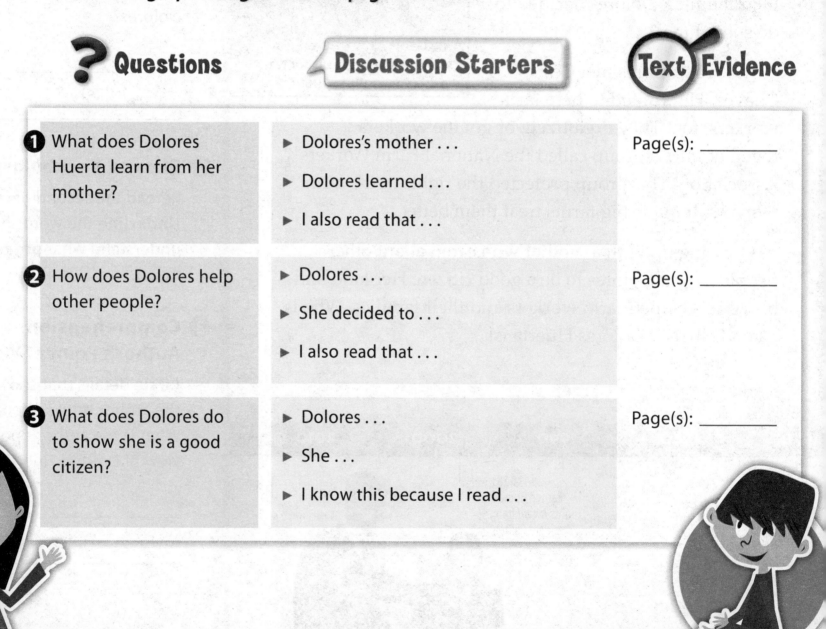

COLLABORATE

Discuss Work with a partner. Use the discussion starters to answer the questions about "Dolores Huerta: Growing Up Strong." Write the page numbers.

? Questions

Discussion Starters

Text Evidence

1 What does Dolores Huerta learn from her mother?

▶ Dolores's mother . . .

▶ Dolores learned . . .

▶ I also read that . . .

Page(s): _____

2 How does Dolores help other people?

▶ Dolores . . .

▶ She decided to . . .

▶ I also read that . . .

Page(s): _____

3 What does Dolores do to show she is a good citizen?

▶ Dolores . . .

▶ She . . .

▶ I know this because I read . . .

Page(s): _____

Write Review your notes. Then use text evidence to answer the question below.

How was Dolores Huerta a good citizen?

When Dolores was young, she learned that _____

_____

_____

She saw _____

_____

Dolores Huerta and César Chávez _____

_____

_____

Dolores Huerta _____

_____

_____

Write About Reading

Shared Read

Read an Analysis **Text Features** Read Ken's paragraph below about "Dolores Huerta: Growing Up Strong." He gives his opinion about how well the author uses text features.

Student Model

Topic Sentence

Circle the topic sentence. What does Ken tell?

Evidence

Draw a box around the text evidence. Is there any other evidence in the selection Ken can tell about?

Concluding Statement

Underline the concluding statement. Why is it a good way to end the paragraph?

> In "Dolores Huerta: Growing up Strong," the author uses a timeline to help me understand more about Dolores Huerta. The timeline shows important things that Dolores did. It tells when she met César Chávez. It shows when she helped pass laws to help farm workers. The author's use of a timeline helps me better understand the events in Dolores Huerta's life.

Leveled Reader

Write an Analysis **Text Features** Write about "Eunice Kennedy Shriver." How well do you think the author uses text features to organize information and help readers understand the topic in Chapter 3?

In _____

I think the author uses text features to _____

_____

_____

For example, the author shows that _____

_____

_____

The author also shows _____

_____

I think these text features _____

_____

Topic Sentence

☐ Include the title of the text you read.

Evidence

☐ Tell whether the author uses enough text features to organize information and help readers understand the story.

☐ Give examples.

Concluding Statement

☐ Restate how well the author uses text features.

Essential Question

What are different kinds of energy?

Go Digital!

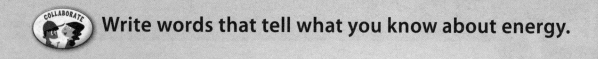

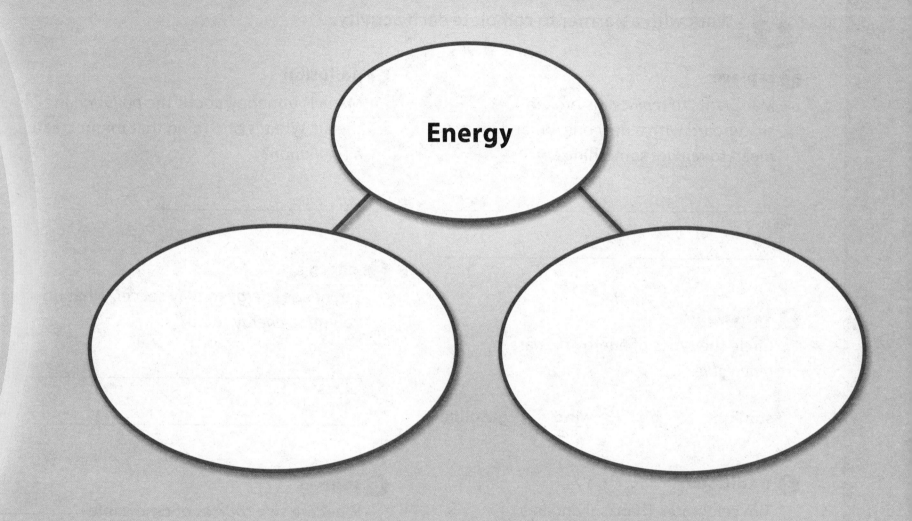

Energy

 Describe one renewable energy source. Use words you wrote above.

Vocabulary

 Work with a partner to complete each activity.

① replace

Mac wants to *replace* his broken skateboard with a new one. What does it mean to *replace* something?

_____

_____

② renewable

Circle the types of energy that are *renewable*.

sunlight   oil   wind   gasoline

③ traditional

Tim celebrates Thanksgiving in a *traditional* way. His family has celebrated it the same way for many years. Circle the words that help you understand what *traditional* means.

④ pollution

Maria is unhappy about the *pollution* in the air. What is one thing that might create air *pollution*?

_____

⑤ energy

Jim needs *energy* to play soccer. What do you need *energy* to do?

_____

_____

⑥ sources

What are two *sources* of renewable energy?

_____

_____

7 **produce**

Chloe banged on a large pot to *produce*, or create, a loud noise. What word means the same as *produce*?

_____

8 **natural**

Draw something made from a *natural* material.

High-Utility Words

▶ **Prefixes**

A prefix is a word part added to the beginning of a word. It changes the meaning of the word. The prefix *re-* means "again."

Read the story. **Circle** words with prefixes.

Jan and Will revisited a wind farm. They wanted to retell what they knew about wind power.

"Wind is a form of energy," said Jan. "It can be reused."

"Wind is also a renewable form of energy," said Will.

McGraw-Hill Education

My Notes

Read "Here Comes Solar Power." Use this page to take notes as you read.

_____

_____

_____

_____

_____

_____

_____

_____

_____

_____

_____

This boy gets his energy from the healthful foods he eats.

Essential Question

What are different kinds of energy?

Read why solar energy is a good source of power.

Here Comes Solar Power

What do people and cars have in common? They both need **energy** to run. Energy keeps things moving.

Energy Today

People get their energy from healthful foods. Most cars get their energy from fossil fuels. These are the **traditional**, or usual, energy **sources** that have been used for many years.

This type of energy is running out and cannot be reused. Once this type of energy is gone, it is gone forever. There needs to be **alternative** energy sources to **replace** them. So scientists are looking for new sources. We need other energy sources that won't run out.

Rey Rich/Aurora Open/Corbis

Text Evidence

❶ Connection of Ideas ⒶⒸⓉ

Reread the first paragraph. How does the author get you excited about reading?

_____

_____

❷ Expand Vocabulary

Reread the third paragraph. **Draw a box** around the words that help you understand what **alternative** means.

❸ Comprehension
Cause and Effect

Reread "Energy Today." The cause is that we need alternative energy sources. What is the effect?

_____

_____

Circle the signal word.

Text Evidence

1 **Expand Vocabulary**

Reread the first paragraph. What does the word **capture** mean?

_____

_____

2 **Comprehension**
Cause and Effect

Reread the second paragraph. What causes a solar panel to produce electricity?

_____

_____

3 **Comprehension**
Cause and Effect

Electricity flows into the house is the cause. **Underline** the effect.

Write the signal words.

_____

_____

Cheaper and Cleaner

Solar power is one source of **renewable** energy. It is not expensive. As a result, many people are using it. They are placing solar panels on their roofs. Solar panels look like big mirrors and they **capture**, or catch, the Sun's energy.

On a bright day, the Sun's rays hit the solar panel. This causes it to **produce** electricity. Then the electricity flows into the house. As a result, there is plenty of energy to turn on lights, stoves, and computers.

The Future

More people are turning to solar power. It's **natural** and is not made, or changed, by people. Solar power is cheaper than fossil fuels and does not create **pollution**.

Today, millions of people around the world use solar power.

Solar panels are placed on a roof.

(b) Holger Burmeister/Alamy; (bkgd) Evgeny Kuklev/Vetta/Getty Images; (r) Cultura Creative/Alamy

GO SUNSHINE!

Solar power is great. Here are the top reasons why solar energy is so hot!

- Solar power is cheap.
- It is renewable.
- It is good for the Earth.
- Power from the Sun is always **available**. It's always there.
- Solar power is natural.

So we should all use solar power. It's good news for the planet!

Paul uses solar power to listen to music.

345

Respond to Reading

Discuss Work with a partner. Use the discussion starters to answer the questions about "Here Comes Solar Power." Write the page numbers.

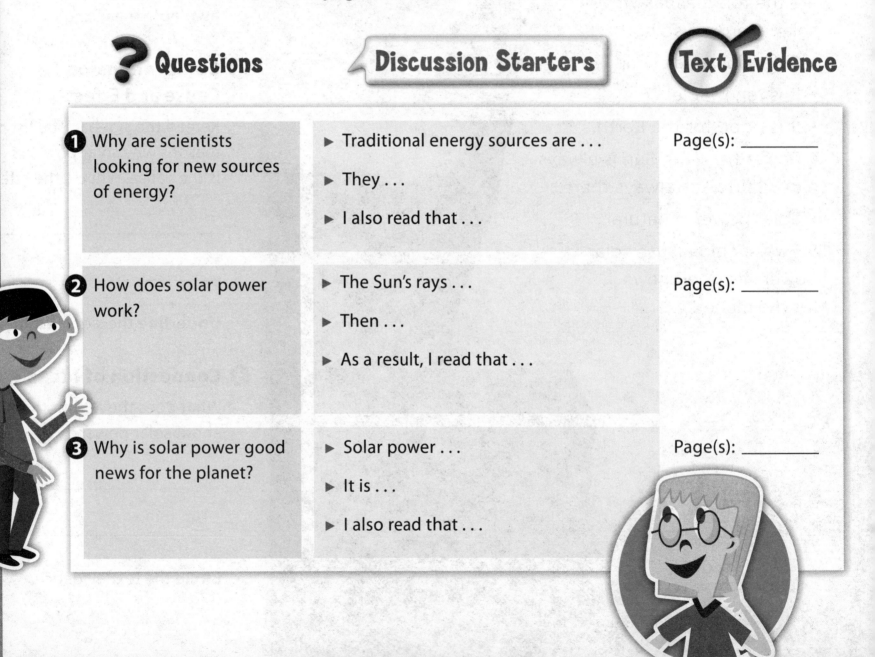

? Questions	Discussion Starters	Text Evidence
1 Why are scientists looking for new sources of energy?	▶ Traditional energy sources are . . . ▶ They . . . ▶ I also read that . . .	Page(s): _____
2 How does solar power work?	▶ The Sun's rays . . . ▶ Then . . . ▶ As a result, I read that . . .	Page(s): _____
3 Why is solar power good news for the planet?	▶ Solar power . . . ▶ It is . . . ▶ I also read that . . .	Page(s): _____

Write Review your notes about "Here Comes Solar Power." Then write your answer to the question below. Use text evidence to support your answer.

What makes solar power a good source of energy?

Traditional energy sources are _____

_____

_____

Solar power can be a better source of energy because _____

_____

Solar power is _____

_____

_____

Solar power can be used to _____

_____

Write About Reading

Shared Read

Read an Analysis **Genre** Read Ted's paragraph about "Here Comes Solar Power." He analyzes how the author uses a text feature to give more information.

Student Model

Topic Sentence

Circle the topic sentence. What does Ted tell?

Evidence

Draw a box around the text evidence. Is there any other evidence in the selection Ted can tell about?

Concluding Statement

Underline the concluding statement. Why is it a good way to end the paragraph?

In "Here Comes Solar Power," the author uses a sidebar to give more information and tell what he thinks about solar power. I read that solar energy is cheaper and renewable. Solar power is also good for the Earth. The author says solar energy can do just about everything. The author uses the sidebar to give reasons why solar power is good.

Leveled Reader

Genre Write about "The Fuel of the Future." How does the author use a text feature to give readers more information in Chapter 1?

In _____

the author uses a sidebar to _____

_____

For example, the author uses the sidebar to _____

_____

_____

It also shows that _____

_____

_____

This sidebar helps to _____

_____

Topic Sentence

☐ Include the title of the text you read.

Evidence

☐ Tell how the author uses a text feature to give more information about the topic.

☐ Give examples.

Concluding Statement

☐ Restate how the author uses a text feature to give more information.

Unit 6

Think It Over

The BiG Idea

How do we decide what's important?

Talk About It

Essential Question

How do you decide what's important?

Go Digital!

Write words that tell about what you value or think is important.

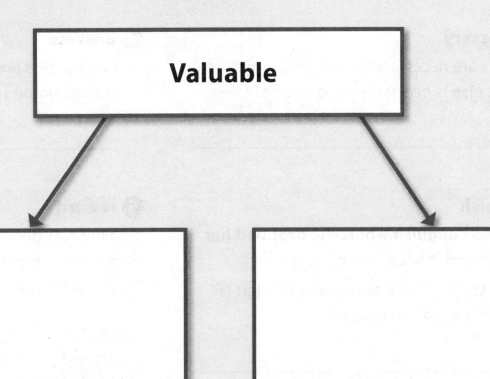

Valuable

 Describe something that you think is valuable or important. Tell why.

Vocabulary

 Work with a partner to complete each activity.

1 **necessary**

Paints are *necessary* for painting a picture. What else is *necessary* for painting?

_____

2 **anguish**

Tess felt *anguish* when she dropped her dollar and it blew away.

Read the sentence above aloud. What is another word for *anguish*?

_____

3 **obsessed**

Colin is *obsessed* with soccer and talks about it all the time. Circle two things someone who is *obsessed* with soccer might do all the time.

play baseball   play soccer

go to soccer games   ride a bike

4 **possess**

Lee's sisters *possess* a big collection of books. Name something you *possess*.

_____

5 **reward**

Jane was given a *reward* for finding her neighbor's lost dog. Tell about a time you were given a *reward*.

_____

_____

6 **alarmed**

Eve was *alarmed* when the dog barked at her. Read the list of synonyms for *alarmed* below. Add one more synonym to the list.

alarmed: panicked, startled

_____

7 **wealth**

The farmer says his land and his animals are his *wealth,* or what he owns. What words help you understand *wealth*?

_____

8 **treasure**

Draw a picture of something you would like to find in a *treasure* chest.

High-Utility Words

▶ **Plural Nouns**

A plural noun names more than one person, place, thing, or idea. Add -*s* to form the plural of most nouns.

Read the passage. **Circle** the plural nouns.

Tony likes to take pictures of spiders. He has many photographs in frames. His friends think the webs look like art. Tony gave his pictures to some of his friends.

My Notes

Read "Athena and Arachne." Use this page to take notes as you read.

_____

_____

_____

_____

_____

_____

_____

_____

_____

_____

_____

_____

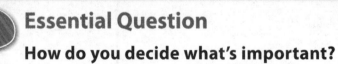

ATHENA AND ARACHNE

? Essential Question

How do you decide what's important?

Read a myth that shows why valuing a talent can cause problems.

Jenny Reynish

CHARACTERS

NARRATOR

ARACHNE: (uh-RAK-nee) a weaver

DIANA: Arachne's friend

ATHENA: a Greek goddess

MESSENGER

═══ SCENE ONE ═══

Athens, Greece, a long time ago, Arachne's home.

NARRATOR: Long ago, Arachne and Diana sat weaving.

DIANA: Arachne, your cloth is so beautiful!

Arachne admires her cloth.

ARACHNE: I know. Many people want to **possess** my cloth. But not many people can **afford**, or have enough money to buy, it. Only people with great **wealth** can.

DIANA: Yes, your weavings are a real **treasure**. Everyone would like to have them. Did the goddess Athena teach you to weave?

ARACHNE: It was not **necessary** for me to learn from a goddess. I was born this way. I am a much better weaver than Athena. I know I could beat her in a weaving contest!

Diana is worried. She stops weaving.

DIANA: Ssshhh! If Athena is listening, then you are in big trouble!

ARACHNE: There's no reason to be **alarmed** or worried. Athena is too busy to compete with me.

Text Evidence

❶ Expand Vocabulary

What nearby words help you understand what **afford** means?

_____

_____

_____

❷ Comprehension
Theme

Underline what Arachne says about the cloth she weaves.

❸ Genre Ⓐ Ⓒ Ⓣ

Reread the stage directions. How does Diana feel after talking to Arachne?

_____

_____

_____

Circle the text evidence.

357

Text Evidence

1 Comprehension
Theme

Reread Scene Two. **Underline** details that tell about what Athena says and does?

2 Expand Vocabulary

What words does Athena say that helps you understand what **boastful** means?

_____

Circle the text evidence.

3 Genre ⒶⒸⓉ

Reread Scene Three. **Draw a box** around the stage directions. What do Arachne and Athena do?

_____

_____

⤚⟹ SCENE TWO ⟸⤙

Athena's home. A messenger arrives.

MESSENGER: Goddess Athena! I have news from Athens. Arachne says she can beat you in a weaving contest. She's **obsessed** with her skill. She thinks she is the best weaver in Greece!

ATHENA: Please get me my cloak.

Messenger hands Athena her cloak.

ATHENA: Arachne cannot talk about me that way! She must say she is sorry, or I will make her pay for her **boastful** and proud words. Her **anguish** will be great!

⤚⟹ SCENE THREE ⟸⤙

Athena knocks on Arachne's door.

ARACHNE: Who is there?

ATHENA: Just an old woman with a question.

Athena is hiding under her cloak. She enters the room.

ATHENA: Is it true you think you can beat Athena in a weaving contest?

ARACHNE: Yes.

Athena drops her cloak.

ATHENA: Well, I am Athena. I will compete with you!

DIANA: Arachne, please don't! It is unwise to compete with a goddess!

Arachne and Athena sit down at the looms. They begin to weave.

Jenny Reynish

ARACHNE: I will win and get my **reward**!

NARRATOR: Arachne and Athena wove beautiful cloths. But Arachne's cloth was filled with pictures of the gods being unkind.

ATHENA: Arachne, your cloth is beautiful. But I am **insulted**. The pictures you weave upset me. Your cloth is mean and unkind. So, I will punish you.

Athena points at Arachne. Arachne falls behind her loom and crawls out as a spider.

ATHENA: Arachne, you will spend your life weaving and living in your own web.

NARRATOR: Arachne was mean and too proud, so Athena turned her into a spider. This is why spiders are now called arachnids. Arachne learned that bragging and too much pride can lead to trouble.

Text Evidence

1 Expand Vocabulary

Athena was **insulted**. What word helps you understand what *insulted* means?

_____

2 Genre (A)(C)(T)

Reread the stage directions. What does Athena do to Arachne?

_____

_____

_____

3 Comprehension
Theme

Reread what the narrator says. What details help you figure out the theme?

Underline the lesson or theme of the play.

Respond to Reading

Discuss Work with a partner. Use the discussion starters to answer the questions about "Athena and Arachne." Write the page numbers.

? Questions

Discussion Starters

Text Evidence

Questions	Discussion Starters	Text Evidence
1 What does Arachne say about the cloth she weaves?	▶ Arachne says . . . ▶ Then she . . . ▶ I read that . . .	Page(s): _____
2 What does Athena do?	▶ Athena . . . ▶ She . . . ▶ Then I read that . . .	Page(s): _____
3 What happens in Scene Three?	▶ Arachne's cloth . . . ▶ Athena . . . ▶ Arachne learns that . . .	Page(s): _____

Write Review your notes. Then use text evidence to answer the question below.

How did Arachne learn what was important?

Arachne says that _____

_____

_____

Athena and Arachne both _____

_____

Athena punishes Arachne by _____

_____

_____

Arachne learns that _____

_____

_____

Jenny Reynish

Write About Reading

Shared Read

Jenny Reynish

Read an Analysis **Literary Text Structure** Read Carol's paragraph below about "Athena and Arachne." She analyzes how the author uses stage directions and dialogue to tell the events in a play.

Student Model

Topic Sentence

Circle the topic sentence. What does Carol tell?

Evidence

Draw a box around the text evidence. Is there any other evidence in the selection Carol can tell about?

Concluding Statement

Underline the concluding statement. Why is it a good way to end the paragraph?

> In "Athena and Arachne," the author uses stage directions and dialogue to tell the events in the play. In Scene One, Athena brags about her cloth. Stage directions tell what Athena does. Then in Scene Three, Athena's dialogue tells about the weaving contest and what happens to Arachne. The author uses stage directions and dialogue to tell about the events in the play.

362

Leveled Reader

Literary Text Structure Write about "Midas and the Donkey Ears." How does the author use dialogue, scenes, and stage directions to tell the story in Chapter 3?

In _____

the author uses _____

_____

For example, the author uses _____

_____

_____

The author also shows _____

_____

These elements of a play _____

_____

_____

Topic Sentence

☐ Include the title of the text you read.

Evidence

☐ Tell how the author uses the features of a play to tell the story.

☐ Give examples.

Concluding Statement

☐ Restate how well the author uses stage directions and dialogue.

Talk About It

Essential Question

How can weather affect us?

Go Digital!

364

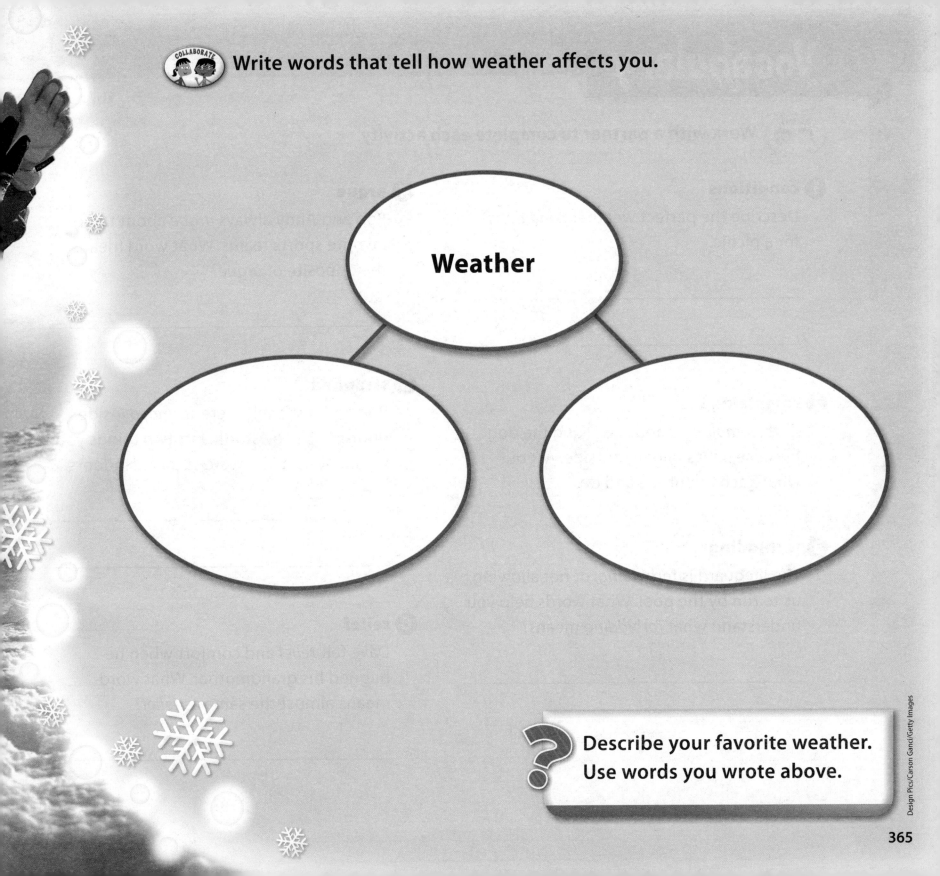

Write words that tell how weather affects you.

Weather

Describe your favorite weather.
Use words you wrote above.

Design Pics/Carson Ganci/Getty Images

Vocabulary

 Work with a partner to complete each activity.

1 conditions

Describe the perfect weather *conditions* for a picnic.

_____

_____

2 complained

Zach *complained* about walking the dog because it was raining outside. Act out what Zach might say and do.

3 forbidding

The lifeguard is *forbidding,* or not allowing, us to run by the pool. What words help you understand what *forbidding* means?

_____

4 argue

Bob and Andy always *argue* about their favorite sports teams. What word means the opposite of *argue*?

_____

5 stranded

Ron and his family were *stranded* inside during the snowstorm. List two things you would need if you were *stranded* indoors.

_____

_____

6 relief

Dave felt *relief* and comfort when he hugged his grandmother. What word means almost the same as *relief*?

_____

7 **astonished**

Cam was *astonished* to see the huge jet land. Act out how to look *astonished*.

8 **forecast**

Draw a picture of what a rainy *forecast* looks like.

High-Utility Words

▶ **Idioms**

An idiom is a group of words that means something different from the meaning of each word in it. The phrase *break a leg* is an idiom. It does not mean to "hurt your leg." It means "good luck."

Read the passage. **Circle** the idioms. Then talk about what they mean.

Lyn and Mike (bundle up) to play in the snow. Lyn's mother tells them to stick together. Lyn gives Mike a hand making a snowman. Lyn thinks making a snowman is a piece of cake.

My Notes

Read "The Big Blizzard." Use this page to take notes as you read.

_____

_____

_____

_____

_____

_____

_____

_____

_____

_____

_____

The Big Blizzard

Essential Question

How can weather affect us?

Read how a blizzard affects a family in New York City.

Stacey Schuett

Rosa and Eddie Hernandez huddled close to the radio and listened carefully to the news.

"The blizzard of 1947 is the biggest snowstorm in New York City history! We are getting large amounts of snow. The weather **conditions** are terrible. Parents are **forbidding** their children to go outside. The weather **forecast** for today is better. The forecast **predicts** that the snow will stop. Everyone should help each other during this big snowstorm."

"Oh, Mamá!" whispered Rosa. "Will Papá ever get home from work?"

Mamá gave Rosa a hug. "He must be stuck at work and can't get home," she said. "He is **stranded**, but don't worry. I'm sure he will be home soon."

Mamá went into the kitchen to make lunch, but came out holding her coat.

"We are out of milk and bread," she said. "I need to go to the market."

Rosa and Eddie had been stuck inside for two days, so they begged to go with Mamá.

"No," said Mamá. "It is too cold."

Text Evidence

1 **Sentence Structure** A C T

Reread the second paragraph. Who is speaking?

_____

2 **Comprehension**
Theme

Reread the second paragraph. What is the message?

_____

_____

Underline the text evidence.

3 **Expand Vocabulary**

What nearby words help you understand what **predicts** means?

_____

_____

Text Evidence

1 Sentence Structure (A)(C)(T)

What details show what Mamá thinks about taking Rosa and Eddie to the market?

_____

_____

Draw a box around the details.

2 Comprehension
Theme

Reread the page. **Circle** the details that show how Rosa and Eddie help during the storm.

3 Comprehension
Theme

What do Rosa and Eddie want to do next?

_____

Circle the text evidence.

Rosa and Eddie knew they shouldn't **argue**, but they were tired of being indoors.

"Please take us. We can all go to the market together," said Eddie.

"Okay," said Mamá with a sigh. "But we have to stay close to each other."

Mamá helped Rosa and Eddie bundle up in their warm clothes. When they got outside, they were **astonished** and amazed to see so much snow. Their neighbor, Mr. Colón, was holding two shovels.

"Who wants to help shovel snow?" he asked.

Rosa and Eddie took turns shoveling. Shoveling was hard work, but no one fussed or **complained**. When they were done, they looked across the street. Mrs. Sanchez was trying to move snow with a small broom. Her market was snowed in.

"Mr. Colón, may we please borrow your shovels?" asked Rosa. "We want to help Mrs. Sanchez."

Shoveling the front of the store was easy for Rosa and Eddie. Mrs. Sanchez was **grateful** for their help. She gave Mamá milk and bread from her store as thanks.

Then, as Rosa, Eddie and Mamá crossed the street to go home, they heard a familiar voice.

"Is that Rosa and Eddie?"

"Papá!" they shouted and ran over to him. Rosa told Papá how they spent the afternoon shoveling snow.

"It's such a **relief** and a comfort to be home," said Papá. "I am very proud of you for helping."

Stacey Schuett

Text Evidence

1 **Expand Vocabulary**

What nearby words help you know what **grateful** means?

_____

Circle the text evidence.

2 **Sentence Structure** Ⓐ Ⓒ Ⓣ

Draw a box around what Papá says when he sees Rosa and Eddie.

3 **Comprehension**
Theme

Reread the details you underlined in the story. How do Rosa and Eddie do what the news report says to do?

_____

_____

What is the theme of the story?

Respond to Reading

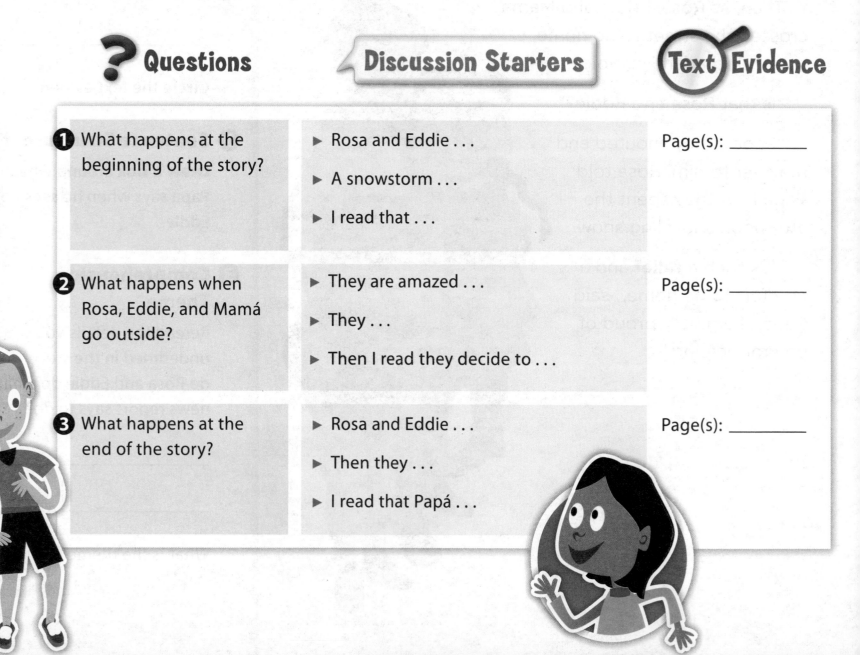

Discuss Work with a partner. Use the discussion starters to answer the questions about "The Big Blizzard." Write the page numbers.

? Questions

Discussion Starters

Text Evidence

1 What happens at the beginning of the story?

▶ Rosa and Eddie . . .

▶ A snowstorm . . .

▶ I read that . . .

Page(s): _____

2 What happens when Rosa, Eddie, and Mamá go outside?

▶ They are amazed . . .

▶ They . . .

▶ Then I read they decide to . . .

Page(s): _____

3 What happens at the end of the story?

▶ Rosa and Eddie . . .

▶ Then they . . .

▶ I read that Papá . . .

Page(s): _____

Mike Moran

Review your notes. Then use text evidence to answer the question below.

How does weather affect the Hernandez family?

A snowstorm _____

_____

_____

Papá was _____

_____

Rosa, Eddie and their mom _____

_____

_____

Eddie and Rosa help _____

_____

_____

Stacey Schuett

Write About Reading

Shared Read

Theme Read Paul's paragraph about "The Big Blizzard." He gives his opinion about whether the author gives enough information to figure out the theme of the story.

Student Model

In "The Big Blizzard," the author uses lots of details about what the characters do and say to show that helping people is important. There is a blizzard. Eddie and Rosa beg to go outside. They help their neighbors shovel snow. The author does a good job using what Rosa and Eddie say and do to help me tell the theme that helping people is good.

Topic Sentence

Circle the topic sentence. What does Paul tell?

Evidence

Draw a box around the text evidence. Is there any other evidence in the selection Paul can tell about?

Concluding Statement

Underline the concluding statement. Why is it a good way to end the paragraph?

Leveled Reader

In _____

I think the author _____

_____

For example, the author says _____

_____

_____

The author also says _____

_____

_____

These elements _____

_____

Topic Sentence

☐ Include the title of the text you read.

Evidence

☐ Tell whether the author gives enough information about what the characters say and do to show the theme of the story.

☐ Give examples.

Concluding Statement

☐ Restate whether the author gives enough information to tell the theme of the story.

Essential Question

Why are goals important?

Go Digital!

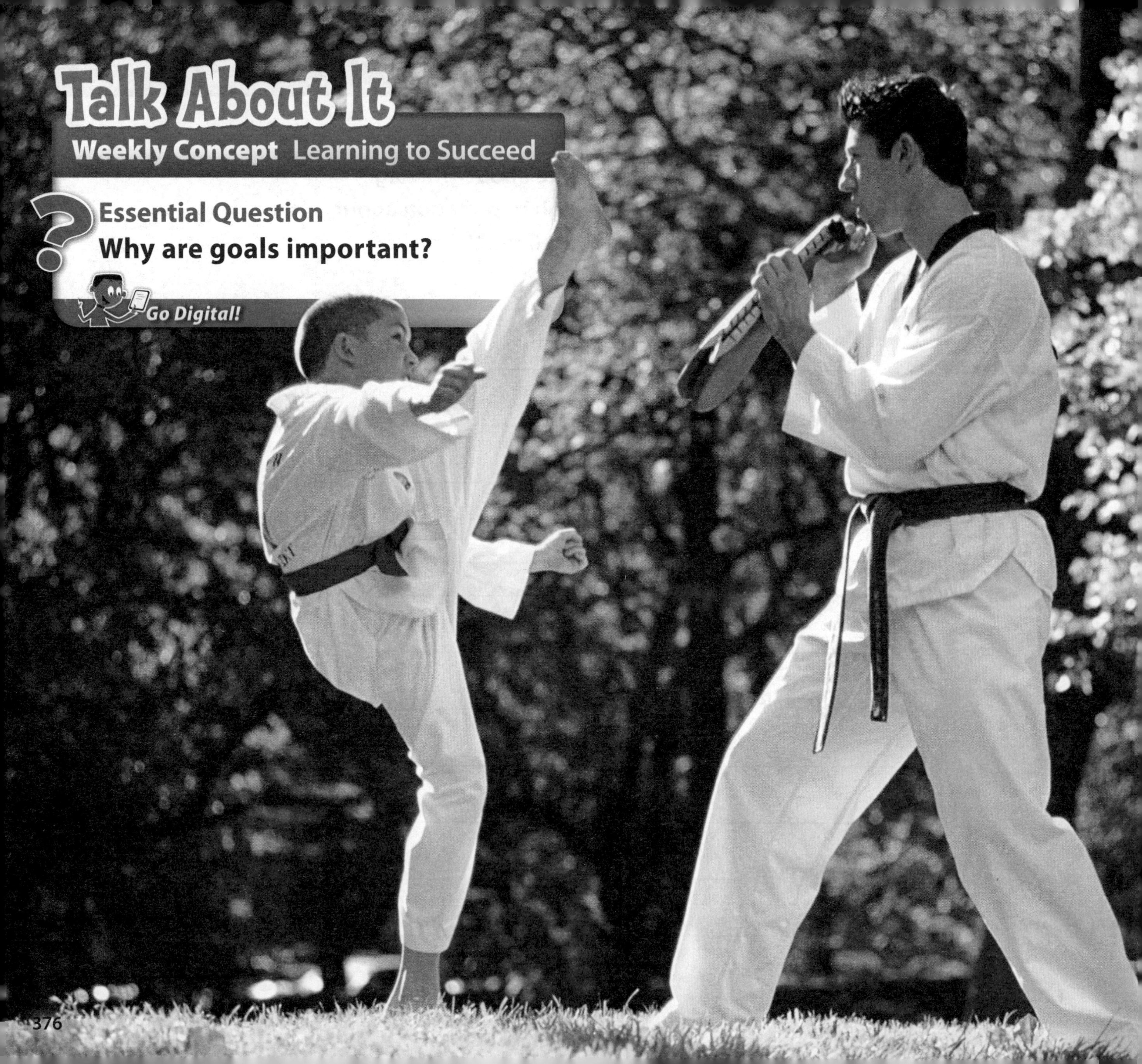

Write words that tell about why goals are important.

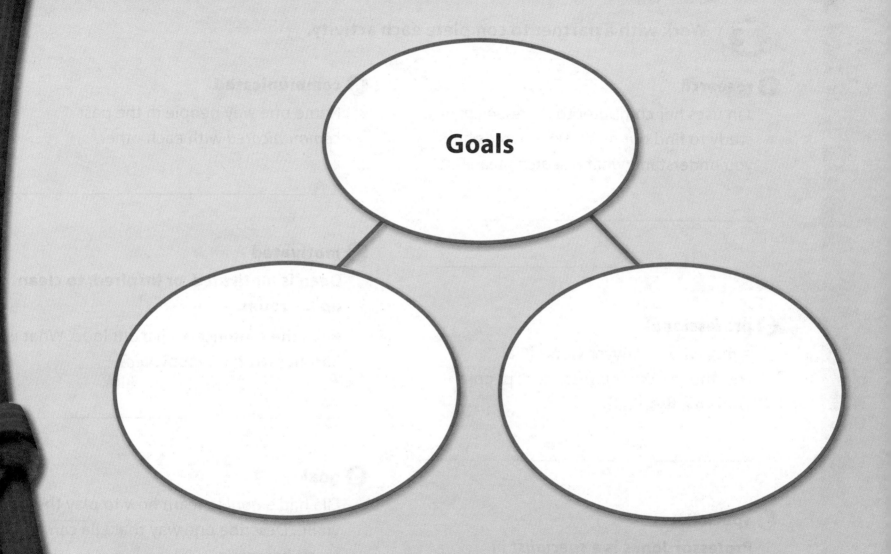

Goals

 Describe one of your goals. Use words you wrote above.

Vocabulary

 Work with a partner to complete each activity.

1 research

Jan uses her computer to do *research*, or study to find out more. What words help you understand what *research* means?

_____

_____

2 professional

A *professional* lawyer works in a courthouse. What *professional* people work in a hospital?

_____

3 specialist

Professor Jones is a *specialist* in American history.

Read the sentence above out loud. If you were a teacher, what area would you want to be a *specialist* in?

_____

4 communicated

Name one way people in the past *communicated* with each other.

_____

5 motivated

Dean is *motivated,* or inspired, to clean up his room.

Read the sentence above out loud. What is another word for *motivated*?

_____

6 goal

Lila had a *goal* to learn how to play the violin. Describe one way that Lila can reach her *goal*.

_____

_____

7 serious

Maura is *serious* about making sure her homework gets done. Act out what Maura needs to do.

8 essential

Draw an *essential* ingredient in sandwiches.

High-Utility Words

▶ **Signal Words**

Signal words, such as *problem, solution, solve, as a result, so,* and *because* show there is a problem and the steps to a solution.

Circle the signal words in the passage.

Jody is learning to play the piano, but she is too busy. She thinks she can solve her problem. She will not watch as much television. As a result, she will have more time to practice.

My Notes

Read "Rocketing Into Space." Use this page to take notes as you read.

_____

_____

_____

_____

_____

_____

_____

_____

_____

_____

ROCKETING INTO SPACE

Essential Question

Why are goals important?

Read about how one man reached his goals.

(l) NASA/JPL; (r) Time & Life Pictures/Getty Images

When James A. Lovell, Jr. was a boy, he loved to build and launch rockets. As he watched his rockets soar high into the sky, he knew someday he would soar, too.

HIGH FLYING DREAMS

Lovell was born in 1928. He worked hard in school and wanted to study space and rockets. Lovell wanted to go to a special college, but he didn't have enough money. He had to find another way to reach his **goal**.

Lovell was **motivated** to find a way to fly rockets. He went to college near his home. Next he studied at a naval academy. Then, Lovell joined the Navy and became a **professional** test pilot. As a test pilot, Lovell flew planes before anyone else was **allowed**, or able, to fly them.

James A. Lovell, Jr. became an astronaut and flew four space missions.

NASA

Text Evidence

1 Connection of Ideas Ⓐ Ⓒ Ⓣ

Reread the first paragraph. What was James Lovell's goal?

_____

Draw a box around the text evidence.

2 Comprehension
Problem and Solution

Reread "High Flying Dreams." **Underline** the sentence that tells about James' problem.

Circle the signal word.

3 Expand Vocabulary

Reread the third paragraph. What word helps you understand what **allowed** means?

_____

Text Evidence

1 Expand Vocabulary

Reread the first paragraph. What words help you understand what **astronauts** are?

_____

_____

2 Connection of Ideas Ⓐ Ⓒ Ⓣ

Reread the first paragraph. **Draw a box** around the reason NASA chose Lovell as an astronaut.

3 Comprehension
Problem and Solution

Reread "Big Challenges." **Underline** Apollo 13's problem. What was the first step the astronauts took to solve it?

_____

_____

PILOT TO ASTRONAUT

Lovell flew jets and taught other pilots how to fly jets, too. He also worked as a **specialist** in flight safety. Soon, the National Aeronautics and Space Administration, or NASA, was looking for **astronauts**. Lovell had all the **essential** skills needed to fly into space, so he applied for the job. As a result, NASA chose him. James Lovell was an astronaut! He had reached his goal.

BIG CHALLENGES

Lovell flew into space three times. Then, in April 1970, he became commander of Apollo 13. This was a big responsibility and a great honor.

NASA's team works to solve Apollo 13's problem.

Apollo 13 was supposed to land on the Moon. But, two days after leaving Earth, the spacecraft had a **serious** problem. One of its oxygen tanks exploded. There was not enough power or air to breathe. The crew could not go to the Moon.

Lovell **communicated** with professionals at NASA. The team did some **research** and found a solution. The astronauts followed the team's directions. They built an invention using plastic bags, cardboard, and tape. The invention worked. It cleaned the air in the spacecraft. But the next problem was even bigger. How would they get back to Earth?

A JOB WELL DONE

The team on Earth thought the astronauts could use the moon module. So, the astronauts climbed into the module and shut the hatch. They had very little power, food, and heat.

The trip back was scary. The astronauts traveled four days in the cramped capsule. They were cold, thirsty, and hungry. Then, millions of people watched on television as the module fell to Earth.

Lovell said that Apollo 13 taught him how important it is for people to work together. His favorite **memory** was when the Apollo 13 module splashed down in the ocean. Lowell said he remembers how the diver knocked on the window to let them know they were safe.

The Apollo 13 crew landed safely on April 17, 1970.

A DREAM COME TRUE

DO YOU DREAM OF GOING INTO SPACE? CHECK OUT SPACE CAMP!

Space camps have been around for more than 30 years. They make science and math exciting. Like the training programs at NASA, these camps teach the importance of teamwork and leadership.

Text Evidence

❶ Comprehension
Problem and Solution

Reread the first paragraph. What step did NASA and the astronauts take to get home safely?

_____

_____

❷ Expand Vocabulary

Reread the third paragraph. Find words that help you understand what **memory** means. Tell what *memory* means.

❸ Connection of Ideas Ⓐ Ⓒ Ⓣ

Reread the sidebar. How are the training programs at NASA and space camps alike?

_____

_____

383

Respond to Reading

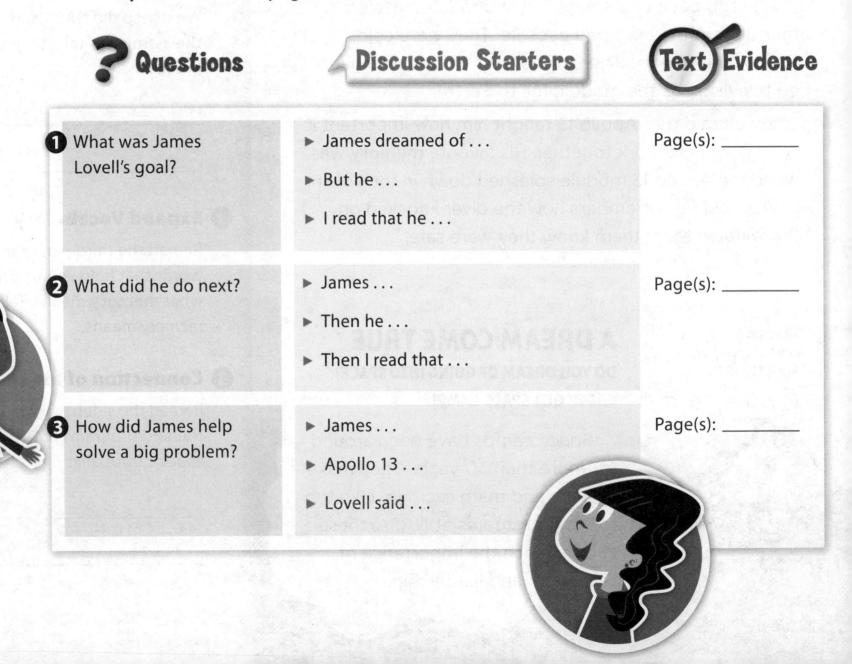

Discuss Work with a partner. Use the discussion starters to answer the questions about "Rocketing into Space." Write the page numbers.

? Questions	Discussion Starters	Text Evidence
1 What was James Lovell's goal?	▶ James dreamed of . . . ▶ But he . . . ▶ I read that he . . .	Page(s): _____
2 What did he do next?	▶ James . . . ▶ Then he . . . ▶ Then I read that . . .	Page(s): _____
3 How did James help solve a big problem?	▶ James . . . ▶ Apollo 13 . . . ▶ Lovell said . . .	Page(s): _____

Mike Moran

Why were goals important to James A. Lovell, Jr.?

When he was young, Lovell _____

_____

_____

He reached his goal by _____

_____

Lovell and his team met a goal during the Apollo 13 mission _____

_____

_____

Lovell said _____

_____

_____

Write About Reading

Shared Read

Problem and Solution Read Tanya's paragraph about "Rocketing into Space." She analyzes how the author uses signal words to show a problem and its solution.

Student Model

In "Rocketing into Space," the author uses signal words to show how James Lovell solved a problem. Lovell and his team went on the Apollo mission. They were supposed to land on the moon, but there was a problem. They worked with NASA to find a solution. They returned safely to Earth. The author uses signal words to show James Lovell's problem and tell how he solved it.

Topic Sentence

Circle the topic sentence. What does Tanya tell?

Evidence

Draw a box around the text evidence. Is there any other evidence in the selection Tanya can tell about?

Concluding Statement

Underline the concluding statement. Why is it a good way to end the paragraph?

Leveled Reader

Write an Analysis **Problem and Solution** Write about "Reach for the Stars." How does the author use signal words to show a problem and a solution in Chapter 1?

In _____

I think the author _____

_____

For example, the author says _____

_____

The author also says _____

_____

_____

These signal words tell us _____

_____

_____

Topic Sentence

☐ Include the title of the text you read.

Evidence

☐ Tell how the author uses signal words to show a problem and solution in the story.

☐ Give examples.

Concluding Statement

☐ Restate how the author uses signal words to show a problem and solution.

Talk About It

Essential Question

How can learning about animals help you respect them?

Go Digital!

COLLABORATE Write words that tell about how we can respect animals.

Respecting Animals

? Describe one way you can show respect to an animal.

Vocabulary

Work with a partner to complete each activity.

1 inhabit

Whales and dolphins *inhabit* the ocean.
Name two animals that *inhabit* the desert.

_____

_____

2 requirement

Sunscreen is a *requirement* for a day at the beach. What is another *requirement* for a day at the beach?

_____

3 endangered

The green sea turtle is an *endangered* animal. Circle two ways we can help *endangered* animals.

play with them   learn about them

protect them   forget them

4 unaware

What prefix do you see in *unaware*?
Underline it. What does *unaware* mean?

_____

_____

5 wildlife

What two words do you see in *wildlife*?
Draw a line between the two words. What kind of *wildlife* lives in the forest?

_____

6 illegal

Miles says that it is *illegal*, or against the law, to throw trash in the street.

Read the sentence above out loud.
What does *illegal* mean?

_____

7 **respected**

Lloyd *respected* his teacher because she was patient. What is another reason someone is *respected*?

_____

8 **fascinating**

Draw a picture of an animal you think is *fascinating*.

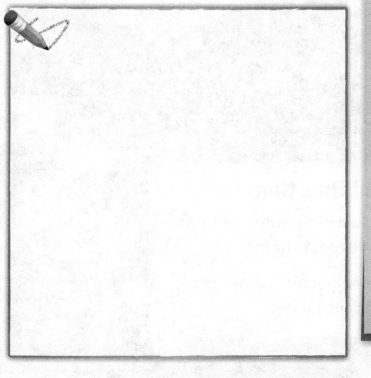

High-Utility Words

▶ **Suffixes with -ly**

The suffix -*ly* means "in a certain way."

Circle words with -*ly* in the sentences below. Write the word's meaning on the line.

1. Stan looked calmly at the bee hive.

_____

2. The bees buzzed loudly.

_____

3. They flew in and out of the hive quickly.

_____

4. Stan bravely watched the bees.

_____

My Notes

Read "Butterflies Big and Small." Use this page to take notes as you read.

_____

_____

_____

_____

_____

_____

_____

_____

_____

_____

_____

Butterflies
Big and Small

Essential Question

How can learning about animals help you respect them?

Read how respecting butterflies can help them survive.

Monarch butterflies like to land in the same trees when they migrate.

(bkgd) Richard Ellis/Contributor/Getty Images News/Getty Images; (r, b) Don Farrall/Photographer's Choice RF/Getty Images

392

There are more than 725 kinds of butterflies flying around the United States and Canada. These **fascinating** butterflies taste leaves with their feet. They only see the colors red, yellow, and green. The Monarch butterfly and the Western Pygmy Blue butterfly are alike in those ways, too. But they are also different in many ways.

Size and Color

The Western Pygmy Blue butterfly is the smallest butterfly in the world. It is about a half-inch across. It is smaller than a dime! Monarch butterflies are bigger. They **measure** about four inches across.

Monarch butterflies are bright orange and black. They are easy to see. Pygmy Blue butterflies are brown and blue. They blend in with their surroundings. Many people walk past Pygmy Blues, **unaware** that they are there.

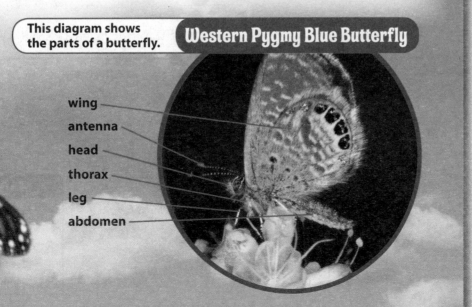

This diagram shows the parts of a butterfly.

Western Pygmy Blue Butterfly

wing
antenna
head
thorax
leg
abdomen

Text Evidence

1 Comprehension
Compare and Contrast

Reread the section "Size and Color." Name two ways the Monarch and Western Pygmy Blues butterflies are different.

Underline the text evidence to support your answer.

2 Expand Vocabulary

Reread the second paragraph. What does **measure** mean?

_____

How big do Monarch butterflies *measure*?

_____

3 Organization A C T

Look at the diagram. What information does the author share that is not in the text?

_____

393

Text Evidence

1 Expand Vocabulary

Reread the first paragraph. What nearby word helps you figure out what **migrate** means?

_____

2 Comprehension
Compare and Contrast

Reread "Moving Around." What is different about the way Pygmy Blues and Monarchs migrate?

Underline the text evidence.

3 Organization Ⓐ Ⓒ Ⓣ

Reread the third paragraph. Cold weather is a problem for butterflies. What is the solution?

_____

_____

Circle the text evidence.

394

Moving Around

Most butterflies **migrate**, or move. The Monarch migrates farther than any other butterfly. It spends summers in the northern United States. Then it moves south in the fall. Many Monarchs travel more than 3,000 miles.

Pygmy Blues **inhabit** deserts and marshes from California to Texas. They migrate short distances north.

Both Monarchs and Pygmy Blues migrate when it gets cold. Butterflies are cold-blooded. They are hot when the weather is hot. They get cold when the weather gets cold. As a result, they move to stay warm. Monarch and Pygmy Blue butterflies also both migrate to find food.

Finding Food

The Western Pygmy Blue butterfly drinks the nectar of many flowers. The sweet nectar is easy to find. Monarch butterflies are not so lucky.

(bkgd) Don Hammond/Design Pics; (b) Mapping Specialists, Ltd.

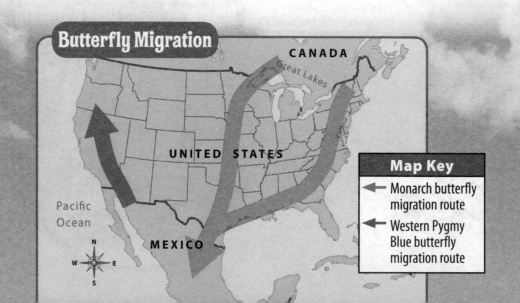

Butterfly Migration

CANADA

Great Lakes

UNITED STATES

Pacific Ocean

MEXICO

N W E S

Map Key
← Monarch butterfly migration route
← Western Pygmy Blue butterfly migration route

Monarchs also drink nectar from flowers. But the Monarch butterfly needs milkweed. It is a **requirement**. Monarch butterflies must find this plant as they migrate.

When people build houses and roads, there are less places for Monarchs to find milkweed. If Monarchs cannot find food, their population will **decrease**, or get smaller. Pygmy Blues and Monarchs are not **endangered**, or at risk of dying out, but biologists are worried.

Help Butterflies

Like all **wildlife**, Monarch and Pygmy Blue butterflies should be **respected**. People can help by planting milkweed and making it **illegal** to destroy their habitats.

Learning about Pygmy Blue and Monarch butterflies is important. We can use what we know to help them live. That way, more people will enjoy them.

This Western Pygmy Blue butterfly stops to eat.

Monarch butterflies feed on milkweed.

Text Evidence

❶ Comprehension

Compare and Contrast

Reread "Finding Food" on pages 394–395. What do Monarchs and Pygmy Blues have in common?

_____

_____

Underline the signal word.

❷ Expand Vocabulary

Reread the second paragraph. **Draw a box** around the words help you figure out what **decrease** means?

❸ Organization Ⓐ Ⓒ Ⓣ

Reread "Help Butterflies." What does the author think about helping butterflies?

_____

_____

395

(l) ©Premaphotos/Alamy; (t) Medford Taylor/National Geographic/Getty Images

Respond to Reading

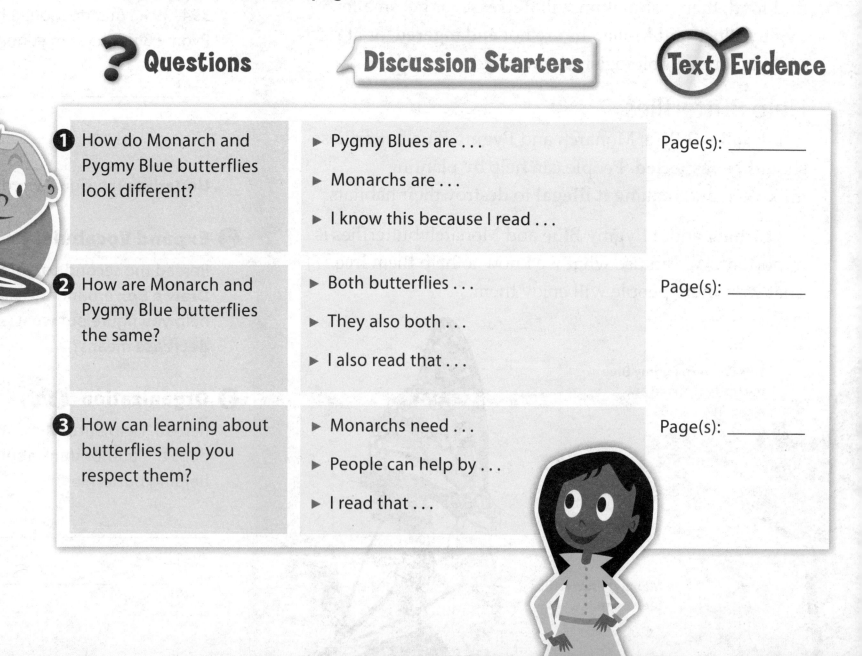

Discuss Work with a partner. Use the discussion starters to answer the questions about "Butterflies Big and Small." Write the page numbers.

? Questions

Discussion Starters

Text Evidence

1 How do Monarch and Pygmy Blue butterflies look different?

▶ Pygmy Blues are . . .

▶ Monarchs are . . .

▶ I know this because I read . . .

Page(s): _____

2 How are Monarch and Pygmy Blue butterflies the same?

▶ Both butterflies . . .

▶ They also both . . .

▶ I also read that . . .

Page(s): _____

3 How can learning about butterflies help you respect them?

▶ Monarchs need . . .

▶ People can help by . . .

▶ I read that . . .

Page(s): _____

Mike Moran

Write Review your notes. Then use text evidence to answer the question below.

How can learning about butterflies help you respect them?

Both Monarch and Pygmy Blue butterflies _____

_____

_____

Monarchs need _____

_____

People can _____

_____

_____

When people learn about butterflies _____

_____

_____

Write About Reading

Shared Read

Read an Analysis ▶ **Compare and Contrast** Read Susan's paragraph about "Butterflies Big and Small." She analyzes how the author compares and contrasts to explain a topic.

Student Model

Topic Sentence

Circle the topic sentence. What does Susan tell?

Evidence

Draw a box around the text evidence. Is there any other evidence in the selection Susan can tell about?

Concluding Statement

Underline the concluding statement. Why is it a good way to end the paragraph?

   In "Butterflies Big and Small," the author compares and contrasts what butterflies eat to explain how to help them. I read that both Pygmy Blue and Monarch butterflies sip nectar from flowers. But Monarchs need to eat milkweed. There are ways people can help. The author compares and contrasts what butterflies eat to show that people need to respect and help Monarch butterflies.

Don Farrall/Photographer's Choice RF/Getty Images

Leveled Reader

In _____

_____

the author compares and contrasts _____

_____

_____

For example, the author says _____

_____

The author also says _____

_____

_____

These signal words tell us _____

_____

_____

Topic Sentence

☐ Include the title of the text you read.

Evidence

☐ Tell how the author compares and contrasts African cats to help explain the topic.

☐ Give examples.

Concluding Statement

☐ Restate how the author uses comparing and contrasting to explain the topic.

Talk About It

Essential Question

What makes you laugh?

Go Digital!

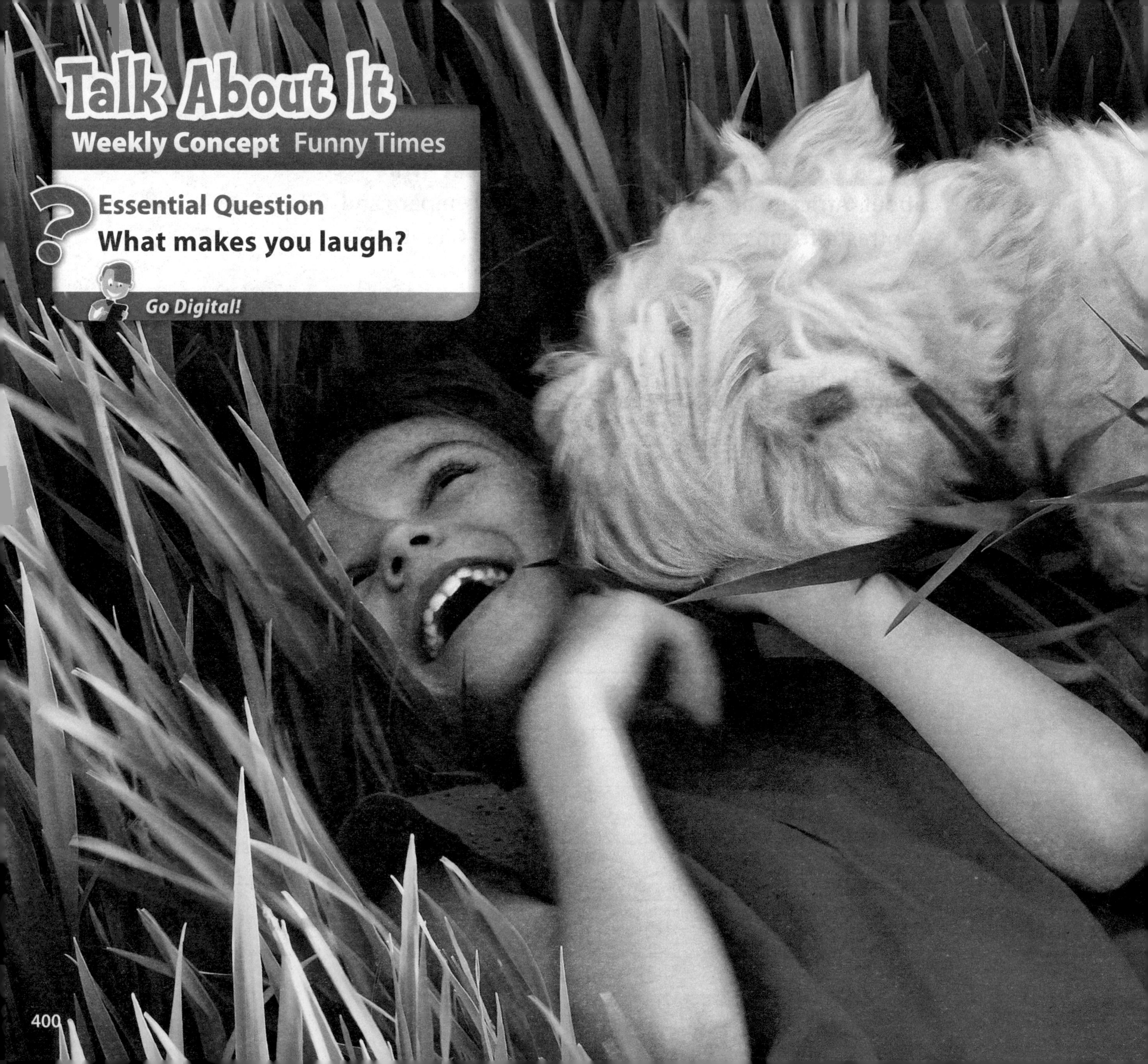

400

Write words that tell about what makes you laugh.

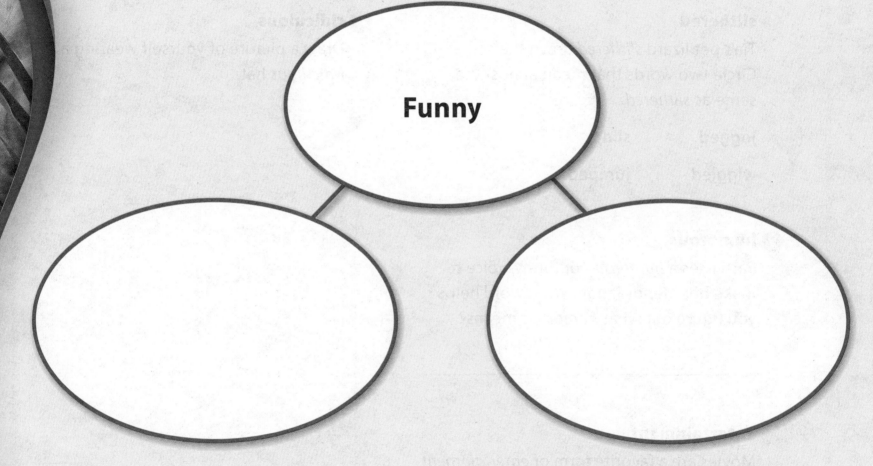

Funny

 Describe how laughing makes you feel. Use words you wrote above.

Vocabulary

Work with a partner to complete each activity.

1 slithered

Tia's pet lizard *slithered* down the stairs. Circle two words that mean almost the same as *slithered*.

jogged   slid

wiggled   jumped

2 humorous

Patti uses a *humorous,* or funny, voice to make her friends laugh. What word helps you figure out what *humorous* means?

_____

3 entertainment

Movies are a favorite form of *entertainment* at Jason's house. What kind of *entertainment* does your family enjoy?

_____

_____

4 ridiculous

Draw a picture of yourself wearing a *ridiculous* hat.

Poetry Words

 Read each poem. Work with a partner to complete each activity.

A Class Game

We played a game in class today.
We answered questions in a silly way.

Maria asked, "What color's the sky?"
"It's purple, yellow and green," said I.

Tony asked, "What color is Lou?"
We all said, "Lou, our hamster, is blue!"

We played the game through all of class,
It made us practice thinking fast.

Our teacher clapped and we were done.
Being silly is so much fun!

5 **narrative poem**

What story does this *narrative poem* tell?

_____

_____

6 **rhyme**

Draw a box around two words in the poem that *rhyme*.

7 **rhythm**

This poem has a *rhythm,* or beat, that makes it fun to read aloud. Reread the poem aloud and clap the rhythm.

8 **stanza**

How many *stanzas* are in this poem?

_____

My Notes

Read the poems. Take notes as you read.

_____

_____

_____

_____

_____

_____

_____

_____

_____

_____

_____

_____

The Camping Trip

We roughed it at Old Piney Park,
With tents and hot dogs after dark.

I'd barely yawned and gone to sleep,
When I felt something creep, creep, creep.

A slimy something crawled on me,
Across my toe, up to my knees

Essential Question

What makes you laugh?

Read two poems about funny things.

Daryll Collins

Ridiculous! Hard to believe,
That creature slithered up my sleeve.

It was not humorous or fun.
I hollered "Rattlesnake! Let's run!"

We all jumped up and stomped around,
Our tent collapsed flat on the ground.

Ten flashlights clicked on to reveal,
That creepy crawly by my heel.

I blushed bright red, "Oops, I was wrong." Snake?

No, a lizard—one-inch long.

—Constance Andrea Keremes

Text Evidence

1 Comprehension
Point of View

Underline details that tell what the narrator thinks. What is his point of view?

_____

_____

2 Literary Elements
Narrative Poem

Reread the third stanza. What happens after the kids jump up and stomp around?

_____

_____

3 Connection of Ideas **A C T**

Explain what happens at the end of the poem. Why is this poem funny?

Circle the text evidence.

Text Evidence

1 **Literary Elements**
Stanza

Draw a box around the first stanza. What words rhyme?

_____

_____

2 **Connection of Ideas** (A C T)

Reread the third stanza. What does the poet compare the narrator's bubble to?

_____

_____

3 **Comprehension**
Point of View

Underline details that show what the narrator's father thinks. What is the father's point of view?

_____

Bubble Gum

I bought a pack of bubble gum,
    As I do every week,
Unwrapping 10 or 20 sticks,
    I popped them in my cheek.

I started masticating,
    That's a fancy word for chew,
The gum became a juicy gob,
    I took a breath and blew.

I suddenly inflated,
    Puffing up like a balloon,
I was a giant bubble,
    Big and round as a full moon.

My father hit the ceiling,
    He was really in a stew,
He hollered, "Stop! Don't go!"
    As out the door I flew.

Daryll Collins

The neighbors' eyes were popping.
    They dropped everything to see.
I was the entertainment of the day.
    Forget about TV.

If you like bubble gum, beware—
    Chew just one stick a day,
Or you'll become a bubble, too
And float up   Up   AWAY!

I saw my friends below me,
    And let loose a mighty roar.
WHOOSH!
All my air blew out,
    And I was just a kid once more.

—Diana Kent

Text Evidence

1 **Comprehension**
Point of View

Underline details that tell what the narrator thinks about bubble gum.

2 **Comprehension**
Point of View

Reread the details. Use them to tell the narrator's point of view.

_____

_____

3 **Literary Elements**
Narrative Poem

Draw a box around the last stanza. What happens at the end of this narrative poem?

_____

_____

Respond to Reading

COLLABORATE

Discuss Work with a partner. Use the discussion starters to answer the questions about "The Camping Trip." Write the page numbers.

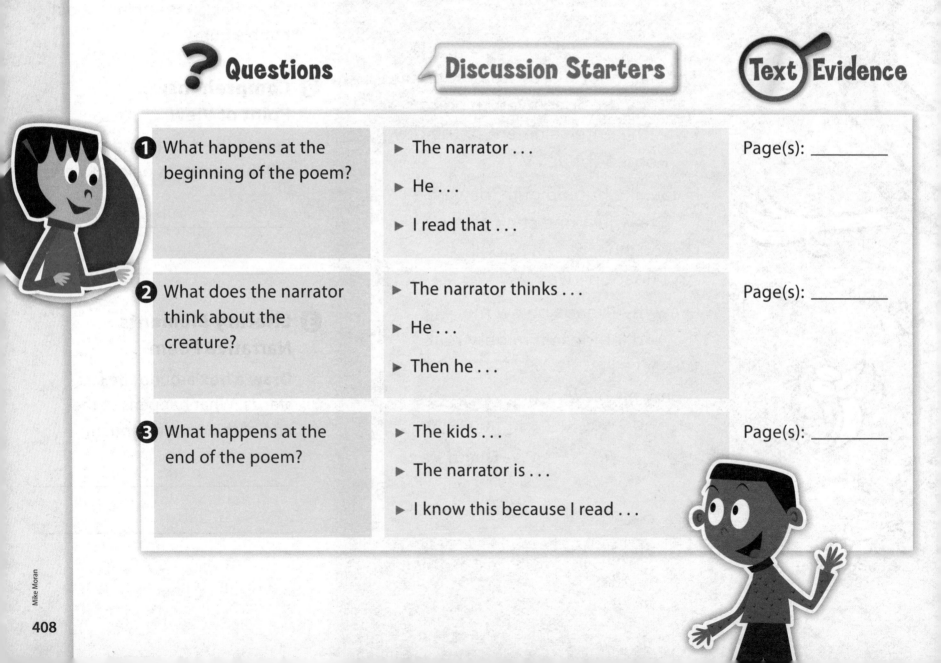

? Questions

Discussion Starters

Text Evidence

1 What happens at the beginning of the poem?

- ▶ The narrator . . .
- ▶ He . . .
- ▶ I read that . . .

Page(s): _____

2 What does the narrator think about the creature?

- ▶ The narrator thinks . . .
- ▶ He . . .
- ▶ Then he . . .

Page(s): _____

3 What happens at the end of the poem?

- ▶ The kids . . .
- ▶ The narrator is . . .
- ▶ I know this because I read . . .

Page(s): _____

Mike Moran

Write Review your notes. Then use text evidence to answer the question below.

How does the narrator make us laugh?

The narrator _____

_____

_____

He thinks _____

_____

The others used their flashlights _____

_____

_____

It is funny when _____

_____

_____

Write About Reading

Shared Read

Read an Analysis ▶ **Point of View** Read Liam's paragraph about "Bubble Gum." He analyzes how the poet uses details to show the narrator's point of view.

Student Model

Topic Sentence

Circle the topic sentence. What does Liam tell?

Evidence

Draw a box around the text evidence. Is there any other evidence in the selection Liam can tell about?

Concluding Statement

Underline the concluding statement. Why is it a good way to end the paragraph?

In "Bubble Gum," the poet uses details to show the narrator's point of view and how it changes at the end of the poem. First I read that the narrator loves to chew lots of gum. She blows a bubble and she floats away. I read that she changes her mind about chewing so much gum. The poet uses these details to support the narrator's funny point of view.

Write an Analysis **Point of View** Write about "Funny Faces." How does the author use details to show the narrator's point of view in Chapter 2?

In _____

the author uses details to _____

_____

For example, the author says that _____

_____

_____

The author also says that _____

_____

_____

These details support _____

_____

_____

Topic Sentence

☐ Include the title of the text you read.

Evidence

☐ Tell how the author uses details about events or characters to show the narrator's point of view.

☐ Give examples.

Concluding Statement

☐ Restate how the author shows the narrator's point of view using events and characters.